Museum Masterpieces:
The Louvre

Richard R. Brettell, Ph.D.

THE
GREAT
COURSES

PUBLISHED BY:

THE GREAT COURSES
Corporate Headquarters
4840 Westfields Boulevard, Suite 500
Chantilly, Virginia 20151-2299
Phone: 1-800-832-2412
Fax: 703-378-3819
www.thegreatcourses.com

Richard R. Brettell, Ph.D.

Margaret McDermott Distinguished Professor of
Art and Aesthetics
The University of Texas at Dallas

Professor Richard R. Brettell is among the foremost authorities in the world on Impressionism and French Painting of the period 1830–1930. With three degrees from Yale University, he has taught at the University of Texas, Northwestern University, The University of Chicago, Yale University, and Harvard University and is currently Margaret McDermott Distinguished Professor of Aesthetic Studies in the Interdisciplinary Program in Arts and Humanities at the University of Texas at Dallas. He is also an international museum consultant with projects in Europe, Asia, and the United States. Recently, he established CISM (Center for the Interdisciplinary Study of Museums) at UTD with a grant from the Elizabeth and Felix Rohatyn Foundation.

His most recent books are *Gauguin and Impressionism* (2005, Yale University Press), *Impression: Painting Quickly in France, 1860–1900* (2001, Yale University Press), *Modern Art, 1851–1929: Capitalism and Representation* (2000, The Oxford History of Art) *and Monet to Moore: The Millennium Gift of Sara Lee Corporation* (2000, Yale University Press). In 2003, *19th and 20th Century European Drawings in the Lehman Collection* for the Metropolitan Museum was published by Princeton University Press, and his scholarly catalogue of *19th Century European Painting in the Norton Simon Museum*, co-authored with Stephen Eisenman of Northwestern University, will be published by Yale University Press in 2006. Dr. Brettell was the guest curator for *Impression: Painting Quickly in France, 1860–1900* for the National Gallery, London; the Van Gogh Museum in Amsterdam; and the Clark Art Institute in Williamstown, Massachusetts (2000–2001). *Impression* was called "the show of the year" by the *London Daily Telegraph* and was enthusiastically reviewed in the *Burlington Magazine*, *Apollo*, *The New York Times*, *Times Literary Supplement*, *The International Herald Tribune*, and all the London dailies.

i

For the past seven years, Dr. Brettell has worked with Elizabeth and Felix Rohatyn, former Ambassador to France, and Françoise Cachin, former Director of the French National Museums, to direct FRAME (The French/ Regional/American Museum Exchange), a coalition of 12 French and 12 American regional museums. Dr. Brettell has lectured at museums and universities throughout the world. He has also served on boards of directors of many national cultural organizations, including the College Art Association, The Georgia O'Keeffe Foundation, the Wendy and Emery Reves Foundation, and the American Friends of the Australian National Gallery. ■

Table of Contents

Table of Contents

Museum Masterpieces: The Louvre

Scope:

The name "Louvre" is instantly recognizable as the most famous art museum in the world. With collections numbering in the millions, it sprawls through a complex of buildings that dates from the 12th through the 20th centuries and covers acres in the heart of Paris—a city that is the art capital of Europe. Many of the millions of annual visitors to the Louvre make what amounts to a pilgrimage to this hallowed museum only once in their lifetimes. They stand in line, negotiate the signs, follow hired guides, listen to a veritable Babel of languages, and leave—a few hours or a few days later—both amazed and exhausted, knowing that their quest to see all that is great in the Louvre is far from complete. Returning to their homes, they nurture memories that are a confused blur of aesthetic sensations that are often difficult to sort or evaluate.

This series of lectures introduces the greatest of universal museums. Its aim is not comprehensive. The focus is narrowed to just one of the seven curatorial departments of the Louvre: the single most famous, the Department of Paintings, which is responsible for European paintings from the Middle Ages until the mid-19th century. These works of art form an encyclopedic summary of the achievements of painters that can be called the single most important such collection in the world. Alone, they require a day of walking to survey adequately; the aim of these lectures is to both prepare new viewers for this visit and to be a "study aid" for those who have been and gone before.

European painting has been considered for centuries to be among the most glorious and complicated modes of expression in the long history of the arts. The Louvre treats that history by dividing the works by national tradition and, within those traditions, by region, school, style, and major master. A patient visitor to the Louvre's collection will be submitted to a crash course in the history of European painting—a course that will form a sturdy scaffolding of visual knowledge that will last a lifetime. The sheer scale and quality of the Louvre's collection of European paintings make it the first required stop on what is, for many, a lifelong study of art. Although the museum's collections include superb French works of the 14th and 15th centuries, it was not until the 16th century that France's embrace of Italian art created the conditions for a truly international aesthetic. From François I, French rulers, whether elected or serving through inheritance, measured themselves against the best works of art produced in other nations, and as the royal collections became more "European," "French" painting became increasingly distinguished. This course will begin with the French rivalry with Italy, which as the national tradition became stronger and stronger, included rivalries with Spanish, Flemish, and Dutch painters, all of whom were collected in France. Each lecture will focus on a small number of major paintings that form a canon of European painting from the 15th through the 19th centuries. ■

Palace to Museum—The Story of the Louvre
Lecture 1

Since its public opening as an art museum in the years following the French Revolution in 1789, the Louvre has become the greatest art museum in the world.

This lecture will give the briefest—and, it is hoped, most enticing—introduction to the architectural complex built over the course of more than eight centuries and covering the equivalent of 30 blocks of central Paris. Visitors have been at once awed and angered by its immensity, its pretensions, and its sheer grandeur. Ultimately no one—not even an educated Frenchman—can ever fully "know" the Louvre, and the first lesson to learn is just that—"Relax, you can never know it all." The second lesson to learn is that, even if you think that you will visit the Louvre only once in your life, plan your visit as if it will be the first of many, choosing to burrow into a part of the vast collections, rather than trying to walk along the surface of an immense artistic landscape.

The Louvre: An Architectural Collage of Two Palaces, One City, and One Museum

The Louvre began as the palace of Philippe Auguste, a walled defensive castle with a circular keep outside the city, built as part of its river defenses. The enlargement of both the palace and the city under Charles V was a gentle fortification with more chimneys and finials than military features. This is represented in *Les Très Riches Heures du Duc de Berry*, the greatest late medieval illustrated book produced in France.

Francis I brought an Italian authority to the Louvre with Pierre Lescot's design to extend the medieval castle, which was built under Henri II. Catherine de Medici, Henri II's widow and regent for her son, planned a vast palace by Philippe Delormes for the Tuileries Palace ("place of tiles") site outside the walls. Again, the monarchy retreated from the city, but this time, on the model of the Medicis' Pitti Palace outside Florence. Henry IV created the first "Grand Louvre" by linking the Louvre and the Tuileries with the Grand Galerie and places of habitation for artists and architects along the Seine.

Louis XIV wanted to build a proper urban palace for the Louvre and hired a series of Italian and French architects to do so. The resulting square courtyard linking Lescot's Louvre with the city was completed by the French architect Claude Perrault with the most impressive and important façade built to that point—and to this day. He also oversaw the complete redesign of the Tuileries Gardens by André le Nôtre. Louis XIV moved the court—and, hence, the capital of France—from Paris to Versailles and essentially abandoned the Louvre as a capital palace, allowing it to become an art school, art collection and exhibition area, artist residency, and center of Parisian royal bureaucracy. Except as an academy, the Louvre atrophied in the late 17th and 18th centuries.

The Louvre: A Universal Museum Rooted in the Distant Human Past

Today, most museum-goers think of art as painting and go immediately to the galleries that enshrine that medium. Yet to the founders of the Louvre as a museum, rather than a palace or art school, it was important to root the collections in the most distinguished—and most temporally and physically distant—civilizations of the past. If France was to be truly a great nation, it had to rival those of the past, and its museum had to contain masterpieces of Mesopotamian, Egyptian, Greek, and Roman art, against which modern people could measure their own achievements. This is a radical notion—that all human history becomes the history of the "French people" and that their accomplishments must always surpass those of every known civilization. Thus, the Louvre presents its viewers first with sculpture—particularly sculpture of the ancient Mediterranean—before it presents painting.

Although the French royal collections contained works of Greek and Roman art before the Revolution, it was not until the worldwide aspirations of the French were made manifest under Napoleon that the Louvre acquired its greatest objects of ancient art. Objects came from three sources: purchases of existing collections, military conquest (resulting in appropriation), and modern archeology. The Louvre was the first truly modern and universal museum—the model for the Metropolitan Museum, the Museum of Fine Arts in Boston, and the Philadelphia Museum.

Featured Masterpiece:
Victory (Nike) of Samothrace (Winged Victory), Hellenistic, 190 B.C.

Discovered by French archeologists in the seaport of the Aegean island of Samothrace in 1863, this extraordinary work of art almost instantly became the symbol of the Louvre. Why? The sculpture is a winged, draped woman without arms or head, but whose thrusting posture and sheer physical energy propel her forward. It is not clear how she was placed in her original setting or even what she was intended to convey; thus, she is symbolically open—able to act as a physical embodiment of inspiration, patriotism, aspiration, and determination.

Corel Stock Photo Library.

The figure embodies a link among water, earth, and air with her wings, feet, and association with a stone ship. Today, she sits as she has throughout the 20th century atop the Daru Staircase, reconfigured and made almost cosmically plain by Andre Malraux after World War II.

I. M. Pei wished to move her to the plinth in the center of the pyramid so that she again would be associated with entrance and so that she would dominate a much more dramatic space.

The Louvre as a Museum Complex

Napoleon created a large courtyard opening to the Tuileries Palace and placed the majority of the national collections in a huge museum—the most important in the world at that time—called Le Musée Napoleon. After 1815, many but not all of the greatest collections of Italian and classical art were returned to their owners. In the 1850s, Napoleon's nephew, the self-styled Napoleon III (Louis Napoleon), hired the Franco-Italian architect Louis Visconti to complete the Louvre, to arrange the destruction of traditional Parisian neighborhoods within its borders, and to increase the size of the museum.

The Tuileries Palace was looted, burned, and largely destroyed by Parisian insurgents during the Commune in 1871. Its ruins stood for more than a decade until its complete destruction just before 1889, the centennial of the French Revolution. The palace was never rebuilt and the gardens became the most important public park in central Paris.

In the late 1980s, the architect I. M. Pei was hired to transform the entire complex of buildings remaining in the Louvre into a single unified museum with underground links. The public entrance was centered in an immense glass-faced pyramid, which took its place in the vast east-west axis of Paris. The overall plan alternates Egyptian and Greco-Roman architectural monuments—the pyramid itself, the Arc du Carrousel (based on the Arch of Septimius Severus in Rome), the Obelisk (brought from Egypt by Napoleon and set up in the Place de la Concorde in the 1850s), and the Arc de Triomphe (built to be seen from the Tuileries Palace by Napoleon).

The Arrangement of the Louvre

The Louvre is arranged into six curatorial departments—museums within the museum: Graphic Arts, Decorative Arts, Painting, Sculpture, Ancient Mediterranean Art, and Egyptian and Near Eastern Antiquity. Each of these has a large curatorial staff and its own galleries.

The Louvre controls more than two million works of art in all media. Sculpture is arranged on the first level in side-lit galleries. Paintings are on the second (and, in most cases, top) level with skylights for equally distributed light. The decorative arts and other objects are shown where appropriate historically. In general, the Louvre is divided between Italy and France, with southern or Italian painting and sculpture (including ancient) on the Seine or south side (entered through the Denon Pavilion) and northern and French painting and sculpture (including medieval) on the north side (entered through the Richelieu Pavilion). Other northern traditions—Dutch, Flemish, and German—are shown with the French. Only paintings from the French Revolution until the mid-19th century are shown on the "wrong" side of the Louvre, in red skylit galleries in which they have been seen for more than a century.

The Richness of the Louvre's Collection

I'm not going to tell you too much about the details of the other collections, but I want to give you a little tiny survey now to show you about the richness of the Louvre's collection. In the Egyptian gallery, the famous bust of Amenhotep IV, the great ruler of Egypt reminds us that Napoleon conquered Egypt, created Western Egyptology, and brought one of the largest and finest collections of Egyptian art to the Louvre. In the Etruscan gallery, the famous *Sarcophagus of a Married Couple* is an excellent representative sample of the many Etruscan works in the Louvre. From among the 300 major masterpieces of Roman and Greco-Roman art purchased by Napoleon from the Borghese family of Rome comes the *Borghese Gladiator* and the *Borghese Hermaphrodite*. Michelangelo's *Bound Slaves* came from the tomb of Julius II. These are arguably the greatest sculptures by Michelangelo outside of Italy. The *Nymphs from the Fontaine of the Innocents* by Jean Goujon, the great French Renaissance sculptor, were on a public fountain in Paris, but were taken off and brought into the collections to protect them. Germain Pilon uses drapery on *The Virgin of the Sadness* to express her sadness and grief at the death of her Son. The *Milo of Croton* is by Pierre Puget, the great sculptor from the south of France, who comes to Paris in the 17th century and makes amazing works of art.

Among the most important visitors to the Louvre, the most frequent and productive visitors have been artists. Artists flock to the Louvre year after year. A look at the work of three artists:

- Hubert Robert was a curator in the Louvre and was involved with the arrangement of the Louvre. He envisioned the glory of what the Louvre could be and painted a premonition of its joining the classical past in ruin. [Project for the Redoing of the Grand Gallery and Imaginary View of the Grande Galeries in Ruins]

- Louis Béroud adored the Louvre and made a kind of sub-profession of representing its light and its mysteries. [La Salle des Sept-Cheminees au Louvre, vue depuis la salle des Bijoux; La Salle Rubens au Musée du Louvre, "A la gloire de Rubens," esquisse du tableau du Salon de 1905]

- Paul Cézanne visited the Louvre hundreds and hundreds of times in his life. Put yourself in his shoes as he stood viewing the Venus de Milo and studied the way in which her body is composed of geometric

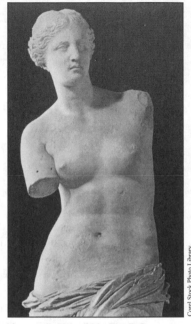

Venus de Milo, 330–227 B.C.

elements; or at the foot of the Bound Slave, by Michelangelo; or at his favorite work of art, Puget's Milo of Croton. [Antique Venus of Milo, Dying Slave, and Milo of Croton] ■

Works Discussed

(Works listed are from Musée du Louvre, Paris, France, unless otherwise noted.)

Unknown Artist (Greek): *Victory (Nike) of Samothrace* (*Winged Victory*), c. 1st century B.C., marble, 10'9" (H).

Unknown Artist (Greek): *Venus de Milo*, 330–327 B.C., marble, 6'6" (H).

Unknown Artist (Etruscan): *Sarcophagus of a Married Couple*, 520–510 B.C., terra cotta, 3'6" x 6'4" x 2'3".

Unknown Artist (Roman), completed by **Gian Lorenzo Bernini**: *Borghese Hermaphrodite*, c. 2nd century B.C., marble, 5'6" (W).

Michelangelo, Buonarotti: *Bound Slaves*, 1513–1515, marble, on the left: 6' 10" (H), on the right: 7'6" (H).

Agasias of Ephesos: *Borghese Gladiator*, 100 B.C., marble, 6'6" (H).

Pierre Puget: *Milo of Croton*, 1671–1682, marble, 8'9" (H).

Edgar Degas: *Mary Cassatt at the Louvre, in front of an Etruscan Sarcophagus*, c. 1880, aquatint, etching, and dry point on Japanese paper, 10.5" x 9.25".

Germain Pilon: *Virgin of the Sadness*, c. 1586, terra cotta, 5'3" (H).

Hubert Robert: *Imaginary View of the Grande Galeries in Ruins*, 1796, oil on canvas, 3'9" x 4'9".

————: *Project for the Redoing of the Grand Gallery of the Louvre*, 1796, oil on canvas, 3'9" x 4'9".

Winslow Homer: *Art-students and copyists in the Louvre gallery, Paris*, 1868, wood engraving, 9" x 1'2".

Samuel F.B. Morse: *Gallery of the Louvre*, 1831–1833, oil on canvas, 6'2" x 8'11", Daniel J. Terra Collection for American Art, Chicago, U.S.A.

Jean Goujon: *Nymphs from the Fontaine of the Innocents*, 1549, marble, 2'5" x 6'5" x 5".

Unknown Artist (Egyptian): *Effigy of Amenhotep IV (Akhenaten)*, 14th century B.C., sandstone, 4'6" (H).

Louis Béroud: *"A la gloire de Rubens," esquisse du tableau du Salon de 1905*, 1905, oil on canvas, 2'1" x 3'.

————: *La Salle des Sept-Cheminees au Louvre, vue depuis la salle des Bijoux*, 1909, oil on canvas, 3' x 2'1".

————: *La Salle Rubens au Musée du Louvre*, 1904, oil on canvas, 6'6" x 9'10".

Paul Cézanne: *Antique Venus of Milo*. Page 27 (verso) from Sketchbook I, 1882–1890. Graphite pencil on wove paper, sheet: 7 ¼" x 4 ¾". Gift of Mr. and Mrs. Walter H. Annenberg, 1987, Philadelphia Museum of Art, Pennsylvania, U.S.A.

————: *Dying Slave*. Page XXVI bis (recto) from Sketchbook II, 1885–1900. Graphite pencil on wove paper, sheet: 8 ½" x 5". Gift of Mr. and Mrs. Walter H. Annenberg, 1987, Philadelphia Museum of Art, Pennsylvania, U.S.A.

————: *Milo of Croton*. Page 22 (verso) from Sketchbook I, 1882–1890, graphite pencil on wove paper, sheet: 7 ¼" x 4 ¾". Gift of Mr. and Mrs. Walter H. Annenberg, 1987, Philadelphia Museum of Art, Pennsylvania, U.S.A.

Suggested Reading

Berger, *The Palace of the Sun: The Louvre of Louis XIV*.

Carrier, *Museum Skepticism: A History of the Display of Art in Public Galleries*.

McClellan, *Inventing the Louvre: Art, Politics, and the Origins of the Modern Museum in Eighteenth-Century Paris*.

Questions to Consider

1. Describe your last visit to the Louvre. If you have not visited the Louvre, what were your past impressions of the Louvre? How have your thoughts concerning the Louvre changed in light of this first session?

2. How would you plan a trip to the Louvre now, after experiencing the first session of the video series? (Be specific and create a plan of action.)

Leonardo and the Origins of the Collection
Lecture 2

These lectures are also about the formation of the collection and the relationship between patrons, kings, collectors, the people who bought the paintings and who thought of them as having a kind-of meaning for France.

This lecture considers the sudden leap onto the European stage of French art during the reign of the French King Francis I in the 16th century. Although France had flirted with the notion of European dominance before this king—and had even managed to unseat the papacy and move it temporarily to Avignon in the 14th century—no single person before Francis I did more to bring France into the Renaissance—and into dominance—than this great ruler. This lecture analyzes his pictorial legacy and deals with his most important artistic act—bringing Leonardo da Vinci, arguably the greatest painter of the Italian Renaissance, to France. This resulted in the Louvre's possession of the single greatest collection of paintings in the world by him. The lecture also explores the state of French painting before Francis I and his court, centered at the hunting palace of Fontainebleau and in the Loire at Chambord.

Other Italian High Renaissance Works in the Louvre

Francis I lived at the height of what has been called the High Renaissance, dominated by three great central Italian artists—Raphael, Michelangelo, and Leonardo. He was able to acquire works by all three, making the Louvre unique outside Italy for its masterpieces by each. Among the 10 paintings in the Louvre associated with Leonardo, two are of the highest level attained by painting in the Renaissance. The earliest, the so-called *The Madonna of the Rocks*, represents the Virgin and Child with John the Baptist and an angel seated in a spectacular landscape, completely unprecedented in Western art.

The second, and greatest, of Leonardo's works in the Louvre is *The Virgin and Child with St. Anne*, begun in 1508. The painting represents an oddly ungainly threesome—the Virgin Mary sits on the lap of her mother, St. Anne, while holding the Christ child on her knee. The infant Christ is playing roughly with a lamb, in an overt reference to his own later sacrifice, and all are placed in a landscape with water and trees in the foreground and fabulous mountains in the background.

The works by Leonardo are rich in ambiguity and psychological tension; those of his rival Raphael are the opposite—clear and calm. Raphael's *The Virgin and Child with St. John the Baptist*, or *La Belle Jardiniere*, of 1507 is everywhere the opposite of Leonardo's *The Madonna of the Rocks*. Although the same subject, Raphael's painting has none of the intensity and lurking danger of Leonardo's. Instead, we see a truly beautiful Virgin seated in a completely benign, light-kissed landscape with a calm sea, a distant church, and delightfully decorative clouds. She caresses her son, who looks at her, while being adored by the appropriately subservient John the Baptist, already given his adult attributes. Few representations of anything in the history of Western art can compete with the calm of Raphael's masterpiece, which likely entered the French royal collections during the reign of Francis I.

Raphael's *St. Michael Victorious* contrasts with his charming *Virgin*. The painting represents the expulsion from heaven of the dragon-like Lucifer by the archangel Michael. Several non-biblical secular texts describe this scene, which shows that dissent occurred even in heaven. Raphael is essentially unable to "represent" evil but, rather, caricatures the demon and allows the calmly assertive archangel Michael to triumph with an almost delightful determination.

The Louvre owns major works by later artists of the Renaissance, as well as masterpieces of the so-called Mannerist aesthete that followed the death of Leonardo in 1519 and Raphael the following year. Examples by Andrea del Sarto and Sebastiano del Piombo (*The Holy Family* and *The Visitation*) only hint at the richness of this highly artificial phase in the history of Italian art.

Featured Masterpiece:
La Joconde (*The Mona Lisa*), Leonardo, 1503–1506.

No work of art epitomizes a museum more fully than does the *Mona Lisa* for the Louvre. Mostly likely purchased by Francis I after Leonardo's death in 1519, the painting has had only two owners in its history— Leonardo himself and the French nation.

Corel Stock Photo Library.

Although there has been much discussion about the identity of the female figure, most viewers accept her as a mysterious smiling woman who was, evidently, the most important muse in the Renaissance master's life. Early in the literature, she was identified as the wife of the Florentine aristocrat Francesco del Giocondo (hence, the French title, *La Joconde*). There are two principal reasons for the fascination we have for this painting. The first is her mysterious quasi-smile; the second is the wild beauty of the Alpine landscape in front of which she sits. Where is she?

French Painting before and during the Reign of Francis I

The mid-14th-century portrait of *John the Good, King of France* by an anonymous French artist shows the extent of primitive Italian influence and the provincial quality of French portraiture in that period. Henri Bellechose's *The St. Denis Altarpiece*, painted more than two generations later in 1416, is similarly provincial. Not until the 15th century did French artists reach an internationally viable level of quality in their work. Two works show the sheer range and power of this newly achieved French tradition in the 15th century—the stronger and more original of which is ascribed to the Provençal painter Enguerrand Quarton. His *Pietà* of Villeneuve-les-Avignons is one of the starkest and most uncompromising representations of this famous scene, made all the more relevant by the painter's inclusion of an intently praying life-size monk. In the last decade of the 15th century, the Burgundian painter Jean Hey, also known as the Master of the Windmills, painted this portrait of Madeleine of Burgundy with her namesake, Mary Magdalene (*A Donor and St. Mary Magdalen*).

There is no doubt that the most important force in French art collecting in the Renaissance was Francis I, who was painted by many great artists, culminating in the greatest of the royal portraits by Titian. The most important French painter of his era was Jean Clouet, who made a splendid portrait of the monarch (*Francis I, King of France*) wearing his usual spectacular clothing and the medal of St. Michael.

The Italian impetus for portraiture is evident in two other works representing contemporaries of Francis I, one of which, Pierre Quthe, was a botanist and pharmacist important enough to have been painted by François Clouet, the son of Jean (*Pierre Quthe, Apothecary*). Clouet represents him in a sober, though richly detailed, velvet and satin jacket over a lace-trimmed shirt. The brilliant green satin of the drapery gives the painting a further luxurious élan. Another portrait, *Flautist with One Eye*, this time by an anonymous artist around the court of Fontainebleau, represents a one-eyed flautist, similarly well dressed, and might be part of a portrait cycle manifesting the five senses, three of which—touch, sight, and sound—are presented here.

In addition to Leonardo, Francis I brought other Italian painters to decorate his palace at Fontainebleau, as well as the chateau in the Loire at Chambord, thought to have been designed by Leonardo himself. These artists hired French and foreign assistants and created an international secular school of painting called the "School of Fontainebleau." These artists, many of whom are still anonymous, were members of one of the largest and most important studios north of the Alps and anticipated the studio of Rubens in early-17th-century Flanders.

Two works from this school represent the sensual secularism of the courts of Francis I and Henry II. The full-length nude, *Diana The Huntress*, representing the classical goddess Diana was painted by one of these unnamed artists in the mid-1550s and has often been thought to have been an allegorical portrait of the royal favorite, Diane de Poitiers. The most alluring of the two works dealing with female sensuality is the anonymous portrait, *Gabrielle d'Estree and one of her sisters, the Duchess de Villars*, presumably of Gabrielle d'Estree with a companion in her bath. ■

Works Discussed

Enguerrand Quarton: *Pietà*, c. 1455, oil on panel, 5'4" x 7'1".

Leonardo da Vinci: *Mona Lisa* or *La Jaconde*, 1503–1506, 2'6" x 1'8".

————: *The Madonna of the Rocks*, c. 1483, oil on panel, 6'6" x 4'3".

————: *The Virgin and Child with St. Anne*, 1508, oil on panel, 5'6" x 4'3".

School of Fontainebleau: *Gabrielle d'Estree and one of her sisters, the Duchess de Villars*, c. 1594, oil on panel, 3'1" x 4'1".

————: *Diana The Huntress*, c. 1550, oil on canvas, 6'3" x 4'3".

Jean Clouet: *Francis I, King of France*, 1530, oil on panel, 3'1" x 2'5".

Raffaello Sanzio, called Raphael: *St. Michael Victorious*, 1518, oil on canvas, 8'9" x 5'3".

————: *The Virgin and Child with St. John the Baptist* or *La Belle Jardiniere*, 1507, oil on panel, 4' x 2'7".

School of Paris: *John the Good, King of France*, c. 1350, oil on panel, 1'11" x 1'5".

Andrea del Sarto: *The Holy Family*, 1520, oil on panel, 4' x 2'7".

Jean Hey: *A Donor and St. Mary Magdalen*, 1490–1495, tempera on panel, 1'10" x 1'3".

Sebastiano del Piombo: *The Visitation*, 1519–1521, oil on canvas, 5'6" x 4'3".

Jean Goujon: *Fountain of Diana*, 16th century, marble, 6'11" (H).

François Clouet: *Pierre Quthe, Apothecary*, 1562, oil on panel, 2'11" x 2'3".

French School: *Flautist with One Eye*, 1566, oil on panel, 2' x 1'7".

Henri Bellechose: *The St. Denis Altarpiece*, 1415–1416, tempera on panel, transferred to canvas, 5'3" x 6'11".

Suggested Reading

Clark, *Leonardo da Vinci*.

Cox-Rearick, *Musée Du Louvre: La Collection de Françoise I*.

Zerner, *Renaissance Art in France: The Invention of Classicism*.

Questions to Consider

1. Explain the formation of the Louvre's collection. How was it created?

2. Describe the impact of Leonardo da Vinci in relation to the Louvre and the history of French painting. Discuss the *Mona Lisa* and his other works in relation to this.

Italian Renaissance and Baroque Painting

Lecture 3

The great French collection of Italian painting [is] a collection that is one of the finest in the world, and was probably the first systematic collection of Italian painting formed north of the Alps in Europe.

The lecture focuses on the immense and varied collection of Italian painting from the medieval period through the early 17th century. Like many other European national collections, the French collections are strongest in Italian painting for the obvious reason that, for everyone in the world, the principal advances in pictorial history occurred in the loosely regulated series of city-states we now call Italy. As we shall see, the French actually measured their own achievements as artists against earlier and, even to them, greater Italian precedents. The lecture deals with a few of the highlights of this collection, from masterpieces by Cimabue and Giotto, the earliest geniuses of Italian art, to paintings by the mysterious 17th-century Italian master Caravaggio. Emphasis is on the "story" of painting told through these collections, as well as the history of the collection both in the French monarchy and in the professional acquisitions of museum curators and directors in the 19th and 20th centuries. Indeed, virtually the entire collection of late Gothic and early Italian Renaissance painting was acquired by the Louvre in the early 19th century by its first great director, Vivant Denon, who, unlike French collectors of his time, was aware of the art historical importance of this painting.

Late Gothic Italian Painting in the Louvre

The two greatest masterpieces of Italian painting from the late 13th and early 14th centuries in the Louvre were seized during Napoleonic times from the Church of San Francisco in Pisa. They entered the Louvre in 1813 and had a significant effect on subsequent French painting and the history of art as a discipline. By Cimabue and Giotto, respectively, they are clear manifestations of the gradual transformation in Italian painting from an anti-illusionist painting based on late Roman and Byzantine traditions to the creation of an independent illusionist realm for the picture, in which space is evoked using a variety of devices, and human figures are fully volumetric and cast shadows.

Cimabue was identified by the first art historian, Giorgio Vasari, as the creator of Italian painting and the teacher of Giotto. This large altarpiece, *Madonna and Child Surrounded by Angels*, is closely rooted in Byzantine traditions. With its space-less gold ground, implacable adherence to compositional rules, and decorative rather than illusionist drapery, it looks backward to a tradition of painting that was more than 10 centuries old when it was painted in the last quarter of the 13th century.It represents the Madonna enthroned in paradise surrounded by worshipping angels and holding the perpetual infant Christ on her lap. The painting transcends time, making no allusions to then-contemporary costumes or jewelry.

By contrast, Giotto's important altarpiece, *Francis of Assisi Receiving the Stigmata* represents the saint, not as an object of devotion for the viewer, but as a devotee himself. Posed in a space-displacing manner, with drapery folds deeply shadowed to reveal the form of his body, he looks up into the sky to the physical manifestation of his vision of Christ, who sends the stigmata of his wounds from the nails of the cross to mark the body of the kneeling saint. Unlike Cimabue, Giotto places this scene in space through his creation of a kind of "set" with an evocation of mountains, trees, a church, and the small hermitage. Beneath the major scene are three smaller pictorial zones, called *predella* panels, that represent: the vision of Pope Innocent II as St. Francis prevents the Church from destruction; the approval of the statues of the Franciscan order by the same pope; and a pastoral scene of the saint feeding birds. All of this, we are hereby taught, resulted from St. Francis's devotion and his vision of Christ.

Italian Renaissance Masterpieces in the Louvre

Fra Angelico ("Brother Angel") was the adopted name of an Italian monk born as Guido di Pietro da Vecchia and known in his Florentine monastery as Fra Giovanni da Fiesole. One of the greatest religious painters in the history of Italian Renaissance art, Fra Angelico painted almost exclusively for the Church, decorating church interiors, the cells of monks, and other spaces in the monastery in which he spent the majority of his working life. This painting, *The Coronation of the Virgin*, like those of Cimabue and Giotto, was seized by the forces of Napoleon in 1811, after having been identified by Vivant Denon, the Louvre's first director, and entered the collections of the Louvre (then the Musèe Napoleon) in 1812. It was originally an altarpiece in the Church of San Domenico in Fiesole, a small hillside town near Florence. The large altarpiece from the 1430s represents the enthroned Christ crowning the Virgin on her entrance to paradise. Surrounding this event are religious and historical figures, who demonstrate both the timelessness of heaven and the depth of human time in Christianity. Throughout the 20th century, scholars have disagreed over its complete attribution to Fra Angelico, with one British scholar thinking that the canvas was completed by Domenico Veneziano.

Two small paintings, one by the Venetian painter Giovanni Bellini and the other by the Florentine master Domenico Ghirlandaio, were made for the private devotion of wealthy collectors and connoisseurs rather than for a church. Bellini's masterpiece, Christ's Blessing, was made in the generation before Giorgione transformed Venetian painting. It situates Christ at the moment of his reappearance after death wearing a garment designed to reveal his wounds and already holding a holy book that prefigures those of the four apostles that were not yet written. Christ's simple humility makes him seem utterly human, and the care with which Bellini painted every aspect of the work makes it seem almost itself an act of worship. The turning of the body of Christ and the directional gaze suggest that it may once have been part of a diptych, perhaps with St. Peter, the Virgin, or the Magdalene worshipping him. The painting entered the Louvre in 1912; it had been in the collection of Prince Orlov in St. Petersburg and, perhaps before that, in the fabled collection of Catherine the Great. The second small panel, *Portrait of an Old Man and Child*, by Domenico Ghirlandaio, has been one of the favorite paintings in the Louvre since it was acquired in 1886 from a Florentine art dealer. Nothing survives to identify the two figures, and because of their anonymity, the painting has always been interpreted as a pictorial investigation of the ages of man. Yet there is no doubt that Ghirlandaio represented a real person, and the sheer quality of the portrait and the almost grotesque features of his warted nose make us yearn to know his name.

The Louvre's collection of the paintings of the Mantuan artist Andrea Mantegna is one of the glories of the museum. Perhaps most characteristic of these is the predella panel, *Calvary,* that was once part of a large altarpiece in the Church of San Zeno in Verona. The entire altarpiece arrived at the Louvre in 1798 but was soon dismantled. The larger central panel and its two wings were returned to Verona, while two of the predella panels that flanked the painting are now in the museum in Tours, France. The sheer majesty of the work is extraordinary, with its columnar figures derived from classical prototypes, its clear perspectival construction, and its bleak landscape setting. The second painting by Mantegna is the *St. Sebastian*, the central panel of a large altarpiece painted about 1480 for the Gonzaga family. It entered the Louvre in 1910. St. Sebastian was a 3rd-century Roman soldier who, after comforting tormented Christians, was martyred by order of the Emperor Diocletian, but later healed by a Christian widow.

Featured Masterpiece:
Fête Champêtre or *Concert Champêtre*, Giorgione, c. 1509

Perhaps the most mysterious painting in the Louvre, this work entered the collections of Louis XIV after passing through the Gonzaga collection in Mantua and the superb collection of the English King Charles I. It may originally have belonged to Isabelle d'Este, who is known to have inquired about buying a work by the artist Giorgio Barbarelli (Giorgione) following his death. The painting has been ascribed to many artists, including Palma Vecchio and Titian, both of whom worked in the studio of the short-lived but brilliant Venetian painter now known as Giorgione. Today, scholarly opinion inclines toward Giorgione himself, although the work may have been completed by either Titian or Palma Vecchio if it was left unfinished at the master's death.

The subject of the painting, called either *Fête Champêtre* ("pastoral festivities") or *Concert Champêtre* ("pastoral concert") has no real precedents in European painting. There are no indications that it has religious significance, and most scholars think that it relates to the pastoral poetry with mysterious and emotional connotations known to have flowered among the aristocracy and intellectuals of Venice.

The featured figures are two clothed courtiers, beautifully dressed and engaged in what seems to be a conversation. They are accompanied by two plump female nudes, one of whom seems to pour water from a pitcher into a well and another who seems just to have stopped playing the flute, perhaps because she has just seen the shepherd and his herd in the middle ground. The landscape setting, from the hilly regions of the Veneto, is lush and warm, but the sky is streaked by clouds, and there is a hint of wind and impending stormy weather. Whether an allegory of the senses or an essay on the fragility of beauty, we will never know, as no document or poetic text has come to light that convincingly explicates the painting's mysteries.

The work has had a profound effect on the history of French painting, and one cannot imagine the 18th-century tradition of the *fêtes galante* from Watteau to Fragonard without it. It is also the single most important source for masterpieces by Courbet and Manet in the 1850s and 1860s, and even Matisse's *La Luxe* is indebted to this work.

Venetian Renaissance and Baroque Painting in the Louvre

Venetian painting has been contrasted with that of northern and central Italy for centuries. While Florentine and Roman artists were seen as obsessed with drawing and composition, Venetians, by contrast, were interested in color, the free manipulation of paint, and a tendency to be dramatic, showy, and overtly emotional. The Louvre's collection has long provided fodder for these historical clichés.

The greatest Venetian painter of the Renaissance was Titian (Tiziano Vecellio), who dominated painting in the watery city during the first three decades of the 16th century. His two greatest paintings in the Louvre are both religious. The earlier of these, *The Entombment*, was painted about 1520 when the artist was in his mid-30s and was acquired for France by Louis XIV. *The Entombment* represents the apostles, accompanied by the bereaved Virgin Mary, carrying the naked body of Christ to the cave that would serve as his temporary tomb. The sheer weight of the body and the existence of a kind of divine floodlight that illuminates it at night make manifest both Christ's humanity and his divinity. Each head is a separate study of grief and intense emotion. The second of the two great religious paintings by Titian in the Louvre is *The Crowning of Thorns*, an immense altarpiece commissioned in 1540 for a church in Milan. It was seized by the French military and entered the Louvre in 1797. The sense of physical activity and motion, of agony and human pain that Titian imparts to the scene is remarkable in the history of art, and his inclusion of the marble bust of the Emperor Tiberius was intended to be a complete contrast with the scene below. Manet and Cezanne made particular studies of this great religious masterpiece, and the former actually painted the same scene in the mid-1860s in homage to the Venetian master.

Two major artists—Tintoretto and Veronese—survived the elderly Titian to dominate painting in Venice in the later 16th century. Tintoretto's representation of paradise in *The Coronation Study* is among the most compelling in the history of art. No ordinary mortals are permitted; Tintoretto represents paradise as a sequence of cloudy floors on which sit various saints, figures from the Old Testament, and other significant figures, as Christ crowns his mother, the Virgin Mary. Though already a large painting, this is a study or visual proposal for an immense fresco in the most important civic building in Venice, the Doge's Palace, decorated by Titian, Tintoretto, Palma Vecchio, and Veronese. Yet even this glorious painting pales in comparison with Veronese's *The Marriage at Cana,* commissioned from the artist for the refectory (dining room) of the Benedictine monastery on the island of San Giorgio in Venice and delivered in 1563. With 134 life-size figures, there is no more splendid Venetian painting in the world than this. When it arrived at the Louvre in 1801, it served as a pictorial model for the great French painter (and Louvre director) Jacques-Louis David when he painted the coronation of the Empress Josephine for Napoleon in 1804–1808.

Caravaggio in the Louvre

The most original and important painter in Baroque Italy was Michelangelo Merisi da Caravaggio, referred to simply as Caravaggio, who burst onto the scene in Rome early in the 17th century and led a famously scandalous and complex life in Rome, Malta, and Sicily before dying in Naples in 1610. His paintings represented the vernacular subjects of the teaming Roman streets, inserting into "high art" a jolt of social and moral electricity from which it would never fully recover. Arguably the most influential painter in Europe after Raphael, Caravaggio had a profound effect on Spanish, Flemish, Dutch, German, and French art from 1600 until 1900.

Of the paintings by Caravaggio and his circle in the Louvre, two are unquestioned masterpieces, and both entered France as part of the collection of Louis XIV. The earlier of the two, *The Fortune Teller*, was painted when Caravaggio was in his 20s. We witness the encounter—most probably in the streets of Rome—between a wealthy and handsome young man and an itinerant female fortune teller. The painting is part of a series of similarly proportioned works that relate to themes of luck, lust, and fortune among the social strata of modern society.

Charles I, King of England, the most important art collector in northern Europe before Louis XIV.

By far the greatest of the works by Caravaggio outside Italy, *The Death of the Virgin* was commissioned from the artist by Laerzio Cherubini for the Roman Church of Santa Maria della Scala a Trastevere in 1605. The painting was rejected by the clergy at the church because the model for the dead Virgin was identified as a prostitute and because the other figures in the painting were associated with Roman street criminals. No less a connoisseur than Peter Paul Rubens arranged for the purchase of the painting by the

23

Gonzaga family, who sold it to Charles I, the first great royal collector of Baroque painting in northern Europe. Louis XIV bought it from a dealer after the dissolution of that collection following the revolution in England. The mute poetry of the painting, its dramatic lighting, and its extraordinary use of drapery to convey emotion make it among the greatest masterpieces of European religious painting of the early 17th century and, to some, even prefigure the religious paintings of the Protestant master Rembrandt. ∎

Works Discussed

Andrea Mantegna: *Calvary*, 1456–1459, oil on panel, 2'5" x 3'1".

——: *St. Sebastian*, 1480, oil on canvas, 8'4" x 4'7".

Fra Angelico: *The Coronation of the Virgin*, c. 1430–1432, fresco mounted on panel, 6'10" x 6'9".

Giorgione: *Fête Champêtre* or *Concert Champêtre*, 1509, oil on canvas, 3'5" x 4'6".

Giovanni Bellini: *Christ's Blessing*, 1465–1470, tempera on panel, 1'10" x 1'6".

Paolo Veronese: *The Marriage at Cana*, 1563, oil on canvas, 22'2" x 32'7".

Domenico Ghirlandaio: *Portrait of an Old Man and Child*, 1490, tempera on panel, 2' x 1'6".

Giotto: *Francis of Assisi Receiving the Stigmata*, 1295–1300, tempera on panel, 10'10" x 5'8".

Cimabue: *Madonna and Child Surrounded by Angels*, 1280, tempera on panel, 14' x 9'2".

Tiziano Vecellio, called Titian: *The Entombment*, 1520, oil on canvas, 4'10" x 6'11".

——: *The Crowning of Thorns*, 1542–1543, oil on canvas, 9'11" x 5'10".

Tintoretto: *Coronation Study*, 1580, oil on canvas, 4'8" x 11'10".

Caravaggio: *The Fortune Teller*, 1595–1598, oil on canvas, 3'3" x 4'3".

——: *The Death of the Virgin*, 1601–1606, oil on canvas, 12'1" x 8'.

Suggested Reading

Bazin, *Louvre Masterpieces of Italian Painting*.

Freedberg, *Painting in Italy, 1500–1600*.

Smart, *The Dawn of Italian Painting, 1250–1400*.

Questions to Consider

1. What role do the Italian paintings in the Louvre play in the museum's collection? Why are they important, and what is the historical significance of the Italian paintings?

2. Which is your favorite Italian painting in the Louvre? Why?

Spanish School of Painting
Lecture 4

It was really not until Louis XVI, the last of the great Bourbon monarchs of France, that Spanish paintings begin to enter into the French royal collection.

T he lecture considers the small but extraordinarily fine collection of Spanish paintings in the Louvre, paying particular attention to the major masterpieces of such artists as Jusepe de Ribera, Estaban Murillo, and Francisco Goya. These works and others were in what was called the "Spanish Museum," established in the mid-19th century before being dispersed, and attest to France's complex relationship—both politically and artistically—with Spain. Through intermarriage, the Bourbon monarchs of Spain were close to the French court in the 18th century, although they had been bitter enemies for centuries before. Although the Louvre does not have Spanish art at the level of the Prado in Madrid; the Kunsthistorisches Museum in Vienna; the National Gallery in London; or even the Metropolitan Museum of Art in New York, the collection that does survive at the Louvre has extraordinary works of art that exerted a profound influence on the greatest French painters of the 19th century, particularly Edouard Manet.

Late Medieval Painting in Northern Spain

Spanish painting of the 15th century embodies among the most potent Christian pictorial traditions in Europe, largely because the Spaniards had just experienced the expulsion of the Muslim "Moors," who had ruled most of the Iberian Peninsula for centuries, and had begun the lamentable expulsion of the Jews to attain a religious purity that remained, in the end, elusive. The Louvre owns two important Spanish late Gothic panels, one by the Catalan painter Bernat Martorell, *The Flagellation of St. George,* a panel of an important altarpiece devoted to St. George. The other, *The Flagellation of Christ* by the Franco-Hispanic painter Jaume Huguet, also a Catalan, sets this biblical scene, not in Jerusalem, but clearly in a setting in the Catalan region, in a then-contemporary building with what appears to be a living king. Both paintings stress the physical violence and pain of religion in ways thought to be utterly "Spanish" in France.

El Greco, the great Greek-born, Spanish painter, was trained in a thoroughly medieval manner in his native Crete, before visiting both Venice and Rome, where he learned about Italian Renaissance art. The painting we see, *Christ on the Cross Adored by Donors*, entered the Louvre's collection in 1908. Painted for a convent in Toledo, Spain, it represents one of the monks and the painting's male donor worshipping the crucified Christ in front of an intensely dramatic, stormy sky, just before Christ's mortal death. El Greco's displacement of the emotion from the body of Christ into the intense darkness of the sky made the painting unique and powerful upon its arrival in the Spanish Museum in the 1840s.

Baroque Painting in Spain

The great Spanish master Francisco de Zurbarán painted scores of altarpieces and devotional paintings for specific religious buildings in Spain and its colonies. His paintings are characterized by dramatic lighting, realistic portraiture, and a simplified Realism. The greatest of his canvases in the Louvre, *The Adoration of St. Bonaventure*, represents the death of St. Bonaventure in the French city of Lyons, where he died in the midst of an ecclesiastical council in the 13th century. Zurbarán portrays him surrounded by James I of Aragon (who was not, in fact, present at St. Bonaventure's death but is mentioned in Zurbarán's source, the Golden Legend), Pope Gregory X, and the bishop of Lyons. These figures are easily identifiable, but it is the wonderfully concise painting of the monks who surround the dead saint that give the painting its nobility and gravity.

Jusepe de Ribera painted this major altarpiece representing *The Adoration of the Shepherds* in just two years before his death in 1652. Painted on commission for the Duke de la Regina in Naples, it was given to the French government in 1802 by the government of Naples. Ribera represents two shepherds kneeling by the holy family in the manger in Bethlehem. At the foot of the Christ child, who lies awake looking up at the larger of the two shepherds, Ribera placed a tethered lamb, evidently a gift to the holy family from the shepherds but acting here as the symbol of Christ's passion. Our sense of the scene's actuality is activated by the figure of the staring peasant woman bearing a gift in the upper right.

The Louvre owns several superb paintings by Bartolomé Estaban Murillo, the most important 17th century painter in Seville and the most highly-prized Spanish artist in France in the 18th and 19th centuries. The great Murillo work entitled *The Young Beggar* was in France by 1769 and entered the collection of Louis XVI in 1782 as one of the earliest major Spanish paintings. Its intense realism and Murillo's evident sympathy for this beggar appealed to French collectors of Dutch 17th-century painting. Louis XVI also purchased the great altarpiece of *The Holy Family* in 1786 from the collection of the Count de Serrant. The softened contours and sweet features of the figures are characteristic of Murillo's late painting. We see the Virgin and St. Elizabeth with Christ and the infant St. John, looking up at a cloudy sky in which God the Father and the Holy Spirit appear to complete the Trinity.

Featured Masterpiece:
The Clubfooted Boy, Jusepe de Ribera, 1642.

Jusepe de Ribera was called "The Spaniard" throughout his long working life, most of which was centered in the Spanish-ruled Italian city of Naples. He was deeply affected by the painting of Caravaggio and the most important Spanish Baroque painter after Velasquez. In 1642, Ribera was commissioned by the prince of Stagliano to paint this life-size representation of a clubfooted beggar in a placeless landscape. The idea of representing someone with no social standing and no clear association with religion makes the painting important, and when it entered the collections in 1869, it was instantly hailed as a masterpiece by realist and impressionist artists.

The boy in the painting stands proudly and poses, activating the sense of self for the viewer. Further character cues come from his forthright position, the crutch on his shoulder, and his toothy smile. He holds a piece of paper in his left hand with a Latin inscription that exhorts us to perform an act of charity, ennobling the viewer for having made the young beggar temporarily happy. The painting relates to a series of beggar-philosophers painted by both Velasquez and Ribera in the 1630s and 1640s that deal forthrightly with intelligence in the midst of poverty and raise questions about both Christian and pagan charity.

Francisco Goya in the Louvre

The greatest modern painter of Spain was Francisco Goya, arguably the first truly modern artist. Although the Louvre does not have a large collection of Goya's paintings, those it has received intense scrutiny from French artists unable to make the Goya pilgrimage to Madrid.

Among the eight paintings by Goya in the Louvre, the finest are his portraits, and of these, the most splendid and penetrating is his 1798 portrait of *Ferdinand Guillemardet*, the perceptive French ambassador to the Spanish court from 1798 to 1800. Guillemardet sits in his chair in an active pose, his legs crossed and his torso turned toward the viewer, almost as if he is in motion. He has an air of alert intelligence that makes the work seem less studied than the formal portrait that it is. The tricolor of the French republic is easily seen, and

Francisco Goya, a great artist in Spain in the late 18th and early 19th century.

we know that the Spanish painter was sympathetic to the radical republican political transformations of France before turning against the country with the Napoleonic invasions in the next decade. The rapprochement between

Goya and the French republic makes this painting appropriate as his great portrait in the French national collection. It entered the museum in 1865, the same year in which Edouard Manet made his trip to see Spanish painting in Madrid.

Goya's full-length portrait of *The Marquesa de la Solana* was painted shortly before her death in 1795 at the age of 38. She stands with a prim reserve in a simple black dress, adorned only by wonderful shoes, a transparent scarf, and an elaborate satin bow in her hair. She seems to be on a stroll but is placed in a setting so simple as to defy identification.Is it a nocturnal landscape or an unfurnished room? Indeed, Goya so reduced the elements of portraiture that we are forced simply to confront the sitter herself, as she confronts us with her odd combination of strength and modesty. ■

Works Discussed

Bernat Martorell: *Flagellation of St. George*, 1435, oil on panel, 3'6" x 1'8".

Jusepe de Ribera: *The Adoration of the Shepherds*, 1650, oil on canvas, 7'10" x 5'11".

————: *The Clubfooted Boy*, 1642, oil on canvas, 5'4" x 3'1".

Bartolomé Esteban Murillo: *The Holy Family*, 1665–1670, oil on canvas, 7'11" x 6'3".

————: *The Young Beggar*, 1645–1650, oil on canvas, 4'5" x 3'7".

El Greco: *Christ on the Cross Adored by Donors*, 1585–1590, oil on canvas, 8'2" x 5'11".

Jaume Huguet: *Flagellation of Christ*, 1455–1460, oil on panel, 3' x 5'1".

Francisco de Goya: *Ferdinand Guillemardet*, 1798, oil on canvas, 6'1" x 4'1".

————: *The Marquesa de la Solana*, 1795, oil on canvas, 5'11" x 4'.

Francisco de Zurbarán: *The Adoration of St. Bonaventure*, 1629, oil on canvas, 8' x 7'2".

Suggested Reading

Brown, *The Golden Age of Painting in Spain.*

Kubler, *Art and Architecture in Spain and Portugal.*

Stratton-Pruitt, *Bartolomé Esteban Murillo (1617–1682): Paintings from American Collections.*

Questions to Consider

1. Why are Spanish paintings collected at the Louvre? Explain the history of this portion of the collection.

2. Choose the Spanish artist featured at the Louvre that speaks to you most. What is most important to you about this Spanish artist?

Rubens and Flemish Painting; Early German
Lecture 5

This lecture is centered in one of the greatest rooms of Flemish paintings in the world, the cycle of immense historical decorations commissioned from Peter Paul Rubens by Marie de Medici in honor of the birth of Louis XIV. Intended for a large room in the Luxembourg Palace, the paintings were moved to a newly designed room in the Louvre in the 19th century. These immense paintings by Rubens and his studio are probably the triumphant masterpieces of Flemish cosmopolitan painting of the early Baroque period. With them, we consider the collection of other works by Rubens and his most important student, Anthony van Dyck, in the Louvre before making a digression into the small but important collection of late Gothic and early Renaissance paintings from Flanders and Germany.

Other Works in the Marie de Medici Series

The arrival of Marie de Medici in Marseille, *The Disembarkation,* records an actual historical event with enormous *éclat*. We see the young princess disembarking from a splendid imperial ship, her black-clad father behind her. She is dressed in white satin with gold embroidery and steps onto the crimson-covered plank to be met by an emissary of Henri IV sent from Paris. In the water at the base of the composition, Rubens represented three hefty nymphs who cavort with a muscular abandon and communicate a lusty joyfulness to the viewer.

The third work *Marie de Medici Reigns in Triumph* is one of the smallest vertical panels in the room, and it represents Marie de Medici as a triumphant imperial queen, dressed in classical robes. Beneath her feet and around her are the symbols of imperial military power.

Rubens received a commission from Marie de Medici, widow of Henri IV of France and mother of Louis XIII, to create an ensemble of immense paintings recording her marriage, the birth of their son, the death of Henri IV, and her regency. The intended location was a large throne room in the Luxembourg Palace. Rubens and his assistants worked on the paintings for nearly five years and they are, with the Whitehall palace decorations in London, the greatest Baroque ensemble of paintings to survive intact. The paintings were brought to the Louvre in the mid-19th century and situated in a room of sumptuous splendor.

In one of the largest and most complex scenes, *The Apotheosis of Henri IV*, the viewers enact their roles as witnesses to a mythic event—the ascension of King Henri IV into a classical pantheonic heaven, lifted almost as a Roman emperor into a pastel-hued paradise of pagan gods.

Rubens's abilities to combine realistic portraiture of actual people with allegorical and mythological figures of similar specificity and his complex organization of figures in architectural and landscape settings are without peer in Western art.

Other Works by Rubens and van Dyck

Louis XIV, grandson of Marie de Medici, continued collecting works by Rubens, and the purchase of *La Kermesse* or *The Village Wedding* added a particularly splendid secular genre painting to the vast imperial scheme commissioned by his grandmother. This painting represents the delightfully drunken revelry of peasants and villagers in 17th-century Flanders. Painted toward the end of Rubens's life in 1638, the painting takes its subject from a tradition of secular morality paintings of the 16th century. This work had a profound effect on French painters of outdoor genre, from Watteau to Fragonard in the 18th century.

Among the most recent addition to the Louvre's great collection of paintings by Rubens is the extraordinary full-length portrait of the artist's wife, *Hélène Fourment*, standing at the entrance to a vast urban palace. This masterpiece entered the Louvre's collection in 1977 in lieu of estate taxes and shows the extent to which important European artists had risen to the highest levels of aristocratic society. In this painting, the artist's young wife is no less pictorially important than was Marie de Medici or the queen of Spain.

Many of the greatest Flemish painters of the generation after Rubens started out in Rubens's studio, but the single most important of those was Anthony van Dyck, who succeeded Rubens as an imperial portrait painter. *Venus Asking Vulcan for Arms for Aeneas* represents a scene from Virgil's *Aeneid*, in which the goddess makes a visit to her husband, the divine blacksmith Vulcan, to order armor for her son, Aeneas.In this splendid canvas of about 1630, van Dyck represents the divine couple at the point of their meeting, with an extraordinarily life-like *putto* in the foreground and the fabulous armor created by Vulcan. It is a visual essay on the art of reconciling opposites— man and woman, peace and war, soft and hard, divine and human.

Works of Older German and Flemish Art in the Louvre

Among the principal masterpieces of Flemish 15th-century painting in any museum, Jan Van Eyck's *The Virgin and Chancellor Rolin*, was commissioned by Rolin in about 1435 as an altarpiece for the cathedral of Notre Dame in the French city of Autun. The painting was among the thousands of works of religious art seized by the government after the French Revolution, appearing for the first time in the inventories of the Louvre in 1796 before physically entering the museum in 1800. In a perfect state of preservation, this painting had remained in the same church for more than three centuries. When it entered the Louvre, painters from Jacques-Louis David to Jean-Dominique Ingres flocked to study its luminous and fastidiously detailed surface. Van Eyck is known today as the instigator of the oil-based medium that gradually replaced egg tempera as the dominant medium of European painting by the end of the 15th century.

The most important pupil of Jan Van Eyck, the Flemish painter Rogier van der Weyden, painted the superb *Braque Family Triptych* in 1451. Purchased for the Louvre in 1913, it features the coats of arms of two great Franco-Flemish families, Braque and Brabant. In the central panel, we see Christ, having returned to Earth from heaven, where he appears with his mother, the Virgin Mary, and his most faithful disciple, St. John, both of whom turn toward him in worship. The heads and upper torsos of the three figures are shown in an immense and perfectly detailed landscape, which continues into the two side panels of the altarpiece.

These wings are devoted to John the Baptist and Mary Magdalene, two humans one step removed from the divine Christ who are intercessors in the act of devotion. All of the figures are dressed as if they are from 15th-century Flanders, bringing Christ directly into contact with the historical present of the painting's creation.

Perhaps the greatest Flemish painter of the early 16th century was Quentin Metsys, whose single greatest painting is *The Banker and his Wife*, which was purchased for the collections of the Louvre in 1806. Once owned by Peter Paul Rubens, the painting is an

Dürer, *Self Portrait*, 1493.

interesting study of early capitalism in its precise representation of a money lender in his Flemish place of business. He sits with his wife and business partner at a counter, on which is arranged a gorgeous still life of metal, glass, and wood objects that were used for examining, weighing, and counting currency. Above them are shelves holding various dossiers and books, on one of which the artist signed and dated the painting to 1514.

In addition to the collections of Flemish art, the Louvre also has a small collection of German paintings, the principal masterpiece of which is the *Self Portrait* by the greatest German artist of the Renaissance, Albrecht Dürer. Painted when the artist was only 22 years old, the portrait is among the earliest indications of the importance of individual artist geniuses in northern Europe. Although the young artist had not yet been to Italy, he represents himself as a beautifully dressed courtier, holding a thistle, an enduring symbol of the passion of Christ. The earliest of the surviving self-portraits by Dürer, this is without question the most important German painting in France.

Holbein, *Erasmus*, 1523.

Among other great artists of the German Renaissance represented in the collections is Hans Holbein the Younger, who worked in what is now Switzerland and later in England for the court of Henry VIII. The Louvre possesses a superb painting by Holbein representing the great Renaissance philosopher and humanist *Erasmus*. Formerly owned by the great English royal collector, Charles I, it was purchased for the French royal collections by Louis XIV and has remained in France as proof of the greatness of European intellectual life to this day. ∎

Works Discussed

Peter Paul Rubens: *The Disembarkation*, 1621–1625, oil on canvas, 12'11" x 9'8".

———: *Marie de Medici Reigns in Triumph*, 1621–1625, oil on canvas, 9' x 4'10".

———: *Apotheosis of Henry IV*, 1621–1625, oil on canvas, 12'11" x 23'10".

———: *The Village Wedding* (*La Kermesse*), c. 1635, oil on panel, 4'10" x 8'7".

————: *Hélène Fourment*, c. 1639, oil on canvas, 6'5" x 4'4".

Hans Holbein the Younger: *Erasmus*, 1523, oil on panel, 1'5" x 1'1".

Jan Van Eyck: *The Virgin and Chancellor Rolin*, c. 1425, oil on panel, 2'2" x 2'.

Louis Béroud: *La Salle Rubens au Musée du Louvre*, 1904, oil on canvas, 6'6" x 9'10".

Albrecht Dürer: *Self Portrait*, 1493, oil on parchment, mounted on canvas, 1'10" x 1'5".

Rogier van der Weyden: *Braque Family Triptych*, 1452, oil on panel, 1'4" x 4'2".

Anthony van Dyck: *Venus Asking Vulcan for Arms for Aeneas*, c. 1630, oil on canvas, 8'9" x 6'9".

Quentin Metsys: *The Banker and his Wife*, 1514, oil on panel, 2'3" x 2'2".

Suggested Reading

Brown, *Van Dyck*.

Millen and Wolf, *Heroic Deeds and Mystic Figures: A New Reading of Rubens' Life of Maria de'Medici*.

White, *Peter Paul Rubens: Man and Artist*.

Questions to Consider

1. What is Peter Paul Rubens's place in the history of French painting? Why is he a significant figure featured at the Louvre?

2. Describe the Old German and Flemish collection of paintings at the Louvre. Which is your favorite piece and why?

Rembrandt, Vermeer, and Dutch Painting
Lecture 6

The greatest artist produced in Holland in the 17th century was Rembrandt van Rijn.

Although not as large as the Dutch collections in Amsterdam, St. Petersburg, or New York, the Louvre's was the earliest major public collection of Dutch 17th-century paintings and includes major masterpieces. This lecture delves into major paintings by the three greatest Dutch artists of the century, Rembrandt, Hals, and Vermeer, although its treatment of the latter two is limited to the close reading of a single work. We will concentrate on the extraordinary group of works by Rembrandt in the French national collections, and reveal the French taste for Dutch 17th-century cabinet pictures that characterized 18th-century Parisian collecting. The lecture also discusses the role of 19th-century French art criticism from the political left on the revival of interest in Dutch art in modern France.

Featured Masterpiece:
Bathsheba at Her Bath, Rembrandt, 1652.

Rembrandt van Rijn was born in Leiden in 1606 and died, already world renowned, in Amsterdam in 1669. During his lifetime, he created about 600 paintings and produced a great number of prints and drawings, all of which are among the world's masterpieces in those media. Because he was famous in his lifetime as an inventive and original artist, many younger painters worked briefly in his studio and, while there and later in their careers, produced works that are similar enough in style to those of Rembrandt that they have routinely been mistaken for the work of the master in subsequent generations.

The Louvre has more than 30 paintings by Rembrandt or members of his studio. There is no doubt that the greatest and most ambitious painting by Rembrandt in the Louvre is the *Bathsheba*. It entered the collection of the museum in 1869 as part of the famous La Caze bequest, which included major works of 17th-century Dutch and 18th-century French art. A visual tour of the painting reveals a wide variety of paint textures, showing how Rembrandt used the tactile dimensions of paint to represent the scene. It is created with intense contrasts of light and dark that seem to represent visually a moral struggle between good and evil. The painting depicts an often-represented scene from the Old Testament that gave European painters an excuse to represent the female nude. In it, Bathsheba, the beautiful wife of an army officer Uriah, is spied at her bath by King David, who seduces and impregnates her. The result of this carnal encounter is one of the tragedies of the lives of both David and Bathsheba and involves the deaths of her infant child and her husband. However, Bathsheba's second son by David was to become King Solomon. The moral complexity of the painting— its failure, in the end, to project a strong positive message—was appealing to modern artists when the painting was first shown in the Louvre. They bridled under the stern rules of a French academy that allowed no such ambiguity.

Selected Paintings by Rembrandt in the Louvre

Rembrandt was perhaps the first great European artist who painted himself throughout his career. The Louvre owns three such self-portraits, including the last from 1660, *Portrait of the Artist at His Easel*. The painting was among the earliest works by Rembrandt to enter French collections, as its second recorded owner was no less a collector than Louis XIV, whose agents acquired it in 1671, just two years after Rembrandt's death.

In painting his self-portraits, Rembrandt costumed himself in various ways, stood in front of the window, and stared into the mirror. Here, he represents himself in the act of painting this very work, serving thus as both artist and model. This small and glowing painting depicts the often-represented New Testament story of *The Supper at Emmaus*. Interestingly, it entered the French royal collections during the reign of Louis XVI, having been in at least two famous French collections already in the 18th century.

No more extraordinary still-life from the 17th century exists than *The Carcass of Beef*. To make it, Rembrandt selected a large wooden panel as the support and situated himself in a shed or a butcher shop, where the flayed carcass of a cow or ox was hung to age from a wooden mount. No attempt was made to beautify the subject, either by arranging it artfully or by introducing other, more easily admirable objects into the scene. It was in Paris in the 19th century and entered the Louvre in 1857.

Hals and Vermeer

Franz Hals spent his entire working life in the city of Haarlem, just west of Amsterdam, and confined virtually his entire career to the art of portraiture.

Hals was best known for a kind of bravura brush work that is not normally associated with Dutch art—which tends toward neatness and a uniformity of surface. By contrast, Hals wielded his brush aggressively—almost as a weapon, slashing across the surface of his canvas. The *Gypsy Girl* is anomalous in Hals's career because it represents an anonymous lower-class girl—perhaps, though not conclusively, the "gypsy" that she has traditionally been called—rather than an identifiable man or woman whose social standing was elevated enough to afford a commissioned portrait. It entered the Louvre in 1869 as part of the La Caze bequest.

Vermeer, *The Lacemaker*, 1669/1670.

Perhaps the greatest rediscovery in the history of art was Theophile Thore's tracking down of the brilliant but shadowy Dutch artist from Delft, Johannes Vermeer, in the mid-19th century. Because Vermeer produced so few paintings (only 34–36 works in his lifetime) and because his career was centered in a provincial town, he was essentially forgotten after his death in 1675 at the age of 43.

Thore, a bit of a visual detective, associated the paintings, then scattered throughout Europe, with each other and with the rare signatures, creating the *oeuvre* of an artist, who, since Thore's path-breaking work, has become a cult figure among art lovers. The Louvre had no paintings by Vermeer in Thore's lifetime and purchased the tiny painting *The Lacemaker* only in 1870. Vermeer's technique is unique in Dutch 17th-century art; a visual tour of the painting—tiny as it is—reveals his profound debt to the Flemish masters of the 15th century that he so admired.

The "Little Masters" of Dutch Art

French collectors began to appreciate Dutch 17th-century painting by the time of Louis XIV, and important acquisitions were common by the reign of Louis XVI, who had a taste for small-scale and refined Dutch cabinet pictures. In French, these artists were called *petits maîtres*, or "little masters," because their subjects were derived from real life and because their works of art were generally of a small scale. The French preferred Dutch artists of a certain type—those who rarely made paintings with religious or historical themes on a large scale.

The earliest and greatest of these little masters was the Leiden artist Gerard (Gerrit) Dou, who worked in Rembrandt's studio but remained in Leiden after the more famous artist moved to Amsterdam. Dou specialized in highly detailed and finished works of art, generally painted on thick wooden panels. Before his death in 1675, his works routinely sold for higher prices than those of Rembrandt. *The Dropsical Woman* represents a sick, wealthy woman who is being attended by her physician and servants as she lies ill.

Gerard Terborch was a painter whose small-scale representations of the lives of the wealthy in 17th-century Holland were among the most prized works in the *cabinets*, or small galleries, of French aristocrats. *The Lute Concert* from 1657 represents an amateur performance, in which one wealthy young woman plays a lute, while her seated companion sings from an original musical manuscript. A young male servant wearing expensive livery brings in a large glass of beer or cider to soothe her voice. The expensive textiles from the Orient and southern Europe in the room attest to the wealth of the family.

The third of the little masters we will explore is an artist who lived and worked in Delft and was closely associated with Vermeer. Indeed, many of his paintings were mistaken for those of Vermeer, in spite of the fact that Pieter de Hooch routinely monogrammed and dated his own works. *Young Woman Drinking* presents two men and two women in a luxurious interior. Because they are drinking and because one of the men wears a hat, indicating that he has come in from the outside, many scholars identify this and similar works by de Hooch as scenes of high-class prostitution in Delft. There is no positive evidence to support these claims.

Terborch, *The Lute Concert*, 1657.

The final painting in this small quartet of refined realist works is by the Leiden-born painter Gabriel Metsu. Of the eight paintings in the Louvre's collection by Metsu, six were in French royal or aristocratic collections, and two, including the superb painting of *The Amsterdam Vegetable Market*, were owned by Louis XVI (this one acquired only six years before the revolution that toppled his regime). ∎

Works Discussed

Frans Hals: *Gypsy Girl*, c. 1628–1630, oil on panel, 1'10" x 1'8".

Gabriel Metsu: *The Amsterdam Vegetable Market*, c. 1660, oil on canvas, 3'2" x 2'9".

Rembrandt van Rijn: *The Supper at Emmaus*, 1648, oil on panel, 2'3" x 2'1".

————: *Bathsheba at Her Bath*, 1654, oil on canvas, 4'8" x 4'8".

————: *The Carcass of Beef*, 1655, oil on panel, 3'1" x 2'3".

————: *Portrait of the Artist at His Easel*, 1660, oil on canvas, 3'7" x 2'9".

Johannes Vermeer: *The Lacemaker*, 1669/1670, oil on canvas, 9.5" x 8.5".

Gerard Terborch: *The Lute Concert*, 1657, oil on canvas, 1'6" x 1'5".

Gerard (Gerrit) Dou: *The Dropsical Woman*, 1663, oil on panel, 2'9" x 2'2".

Pieter de Hooch: *Young Woman Drinking*, 1658, oil on canvas, 2'3" x 1'11".

Suggested Reading

Alpers, *The Art of Describing Dutch Art*.

Brown, *Rembrandt*.

Schama, *The Embarrassment of Riches: An Interpretation of Dutch Culture in the Golden Age*.

Questions to Consider

1. How is Rembrandt represented in the Louvre's collection, and why is he important to the story of the history of Western art?

2. Choose a painting from one the Dutch masters. What is its significance to you, and why is it important to the Louvre's collected works?

De La Tour, Le Nain, and 17ᵗʰ-Century Painting
Lecture 7

We're going to begin now in the 17ᵗʰ century, in the so-called "*Le Grand Siecle*" as it's called in French ("The Great Century"), in which French art and particularly French painting attained a very high international level.

This lecture focuses on the careers of Georges de La Tour, the most profoundly original French painter of the first half of the 17ᵗʰ century, and the Le Nain brothers, who created a completely new kind of painting in France. The work of these "indigenous" French artists is then contrasted with the work of equally "French" artists who were trained in Italy and whose work can be read as an extension of Italian Baroque aesthetics applied to French contexts. The lecture also contrasts works made to evoke France in all its regional glory with those created for Paris and its elites. In closing, the lecture looks at the creation of the French Academy under Louis XIV and the role of the visual arts in establishing French cultural preeminence vis-à-vis Italy.

Georges de La Tour

The Louvre has the single largest and finest collection of works by Georges de La Tour in the world. The four works chosen for discussion here are all religious paintings; three have New Testament subjects, and one derives from the post-biblical lives of the Christian saints. All but one seems to have been painted for display in the secular spaces of city homes or chateaux rather than in churches.

The earliest of the group, probably painted between 1630 and 1635, is his representation of *The Penitent Mary Magdalen*, a subject de La Tour repeated in several variants with marvelously subtle transformations. Unlike *The Cheat*, this painting seems to be about the interplay of light and darkness and is, hence, one of his extraordinary nocturnes. Rather than represent the famous biblical courtesan in the luxurious clothes and jewelry in which she is often represented in Italian art, de La Tour selected a young woman who is dressed in simple clothes and sits at a book-strewn table with a human skull in her lap. The tall flame that lights the painting illuminates her bare shoulders, revealing enough flesh to suggest that she is not a "virtuous woman." However, her silent meditation on morality and death is so persuasive that we have no choice but to join her in reflecting on a visual and spiritual quest. The seriousness and simplicity of the painting are de La Tour hallmarks.

The first major work by Georges de La Tour to enter the Louvre was *The Adoration of the Shepherds*, painted in the 1640s. When purchased in 1926, it was an official French response to the German art historian who had resuscitated the great artist's reputation. Most artists in the history of Western art represent this scene out-of-doors and include the animals of the visiting shepherds, but de La Tour compresses the humans into a group huddled around the Christ child. On one side of Christ is Mary, clad in a brilliant red that is a chromatic prefiguration of Christ's death and the incarnation. On the other side is St. Joseph, who directs the light of an unseen candle onto the swaddled body of the infant, a representation that differs from others in which the infant is unclothed. We can see that de La Tour used a small group of models for his various figures over and over, and it is possible that the young woman who modeled for the Virgin Mary is the same full-faced young woman who had been his Mary Magdalene.

de La Tour, *The Adoration of the Shepherds*, c. 1644.

St. Joseph, who was to serve a selfless role as the human father of the divine Jesus, is most represented in the history of art as a secondary figure, with a lesser pictorial and textual role than the Virgin Mary. De La Tour was fascinated by Joseph, and one of his greatest and most original paintings, *St. Joseph the Carpenter*, represents this virtuous figure at work, with his young son looking on. The fact that the older man is working at night shows his sheer devotion, and we admire the young Jesus all the more because he stays up to light his human father's work. De La Tour employs the same model for Joseph as in the previous painting, showing a family connection among his works. As is usual for the artist, the figures seem to bend down to fit into the painting. If they stood up, they would not fit into its confines.

The largest and most complex of the paintings by de La Tour in the Louvre represents a post-biblical scene of the Roman widow Irene removing the arrows from the nearly lifeless body of the martyred St. Sebastian [*St. Sebastian Tended by St. Irene*]. Here again, de La Tour's originality is marked. Most artists represent the saint standing, his body riddled with the arrows of his Roman captors. Here, we see him left for dead, when his body was discovered by fellow Christians, who minister to him. This painting from the last years of the artist's life is also his most complex composition. Its vertical format and large scale indicate that it was most probably an altarpiece commissioned for a particular church, which has not yet been identified. Acquired by the Louvre in 1979, this is the most recent work by this great artist to enter the Louvre, more than 300 years after his death.

Featured Masterpiece:
The Cheat With the Ace of Diamonds,
Georges de La Tour, 1635.

Little is known about the career of Georges de La Tour. His distinctive style derives from the impetus of the Italian Baroque Realist Caravaggio, yet we have no proof that the painter ever visited Italy. De La Tour was born in Vic-sur-Seille in 1593 and died in 1652 in Luneville, where he seems to have painted for most of his life. He appears to have been self-taught, but by the time of his appointment as painter to the court of Louis XIII in 1639, he had become familiar with the work of Caravaggio and his numerous northern followers. His particular brand of Caravaggism is unique in its geometric simplification of form and poetic use of light.

The Cheat derives both its horizontal format and composition from the work of Caravaggio, who also painted genre scenes with life-size figures that represent modern moral foibles and their consequences. Probably dating from the 1630s, *The Cheat* was signed by the artist but left undated, as was his custom. Like all the major paintings by de La Tour in the Louvre, it entered the museum in the 20th century, when his work began to be actively studied. Indeed, following his death in 1652, his work fell into disfavor and was not rediscovered until 1915 by a German art historian, who created a provisional list of signed and ascribed works. Hence, de La Tour is a "modern" rediscovery.

A visual tour of the painting—from the interplay of ovals in the eyes, face, and jewelry of the central female figure to the glorious representation of metal and luxurious textiles—reveals a technical *tour de force*. The subject of the painting cannot be clearly ascertained because we know nothing about the intentions of the owner. The drama is effortlessly played out, and the painting is readily accessible. We can easily read the situation in which a gorgeously dressed young man is being systematically fleeced of his money by experienced cheaters.

The viewer seems to play a double role, as either a knowing voyeur or the fourth card player. It is a painting that would have appealed to an urban clientele.

De La Tour's paintings are so distilled and perfect that he was frequently asked to make replicas or variants of them for other clients. The Kimbell Art Museum in Fort Worth, Texas, has an autographed variant, *The Card Cheat With the Ace of Clubs*, which is painted on a canvas of more pronounced horizontality, thereby compressing the scene and forcing our attention to the sly mechanics of the cheaters. Although the date has not been confirmed, the painting in the Louvre is likely the earlier one, as it has more *pentimenti*, or "little changes," than the other version.

The Le Nain Brothers

Born between 1598 and 1610 in the northern French cathedral town of Laon, the Le Nain brothers, Louis, Antoine, and Mathieu, were all in Paris by 1630 and worked as painters of rural subjects in the capital until their deaths— Louis and Antoine in 1648 and Mathieu in 1672. Although various attempts have been made to distinguish their works into those of three separate "hands," this has proven difficult, because they remained unmarried, worked in the same studio, and often collaborated. This does not mean that their work is stylistically uniform, or that we cannot point to clear subgroups of stylistically similar works.

The Louvre collection of works by Le Nain is, without question, the greatest in the world, but major paintings by the brothers are also found in England and in the United States. The two paintings we discuss are similar in only one way—they represent people who have always been identified as peasants with no attempt at historical or religious overlay. The more often reproduced of the two, the *Peasant Meal*, represents nine figures, probably a family, posed in a humble domestic interior. They seem utterly aware of the painter-viewer, as if they have adjusted themselves to sit for a portrait. In this awareness, the work is startlingly original, because the very fact that they pose gives the figures the same kind of dignity that is assumed by the wealthy when they sit for portraits. As viewers, we know that these people could never afford an expensive painting. The gray and beige tonalities, the superb still-life elements, the seemingly wise animals—in particular, the little dog—are completely original to the Le Nain brothers. The Louvre acquired the painting in 1915.

The second painting, *The Car,* or *The Return from Haymaking*, sets three separate groups of rural workers into a landscape with a tumble-down barn, a mound of newly-cut hay, and wooden tools. This painting is as visually disjointed and blond as the interior scene is compositionally unified and gray, but each represents rural people as if they are posing to be painted. This work is the bolder and more original of the two and has fascinated artist visitors to the Louvre since its acquisition in 1879. One cannot imagine the later rural paintings of Pissarro or Gauguin without it.

Italian Traditions in French Painting

Simon Vouet was perhaps the first great French artist who painted *en par* with the masters of Italian Baroque painting. Born in Paris in 1590, Vouet died in there in 1649, a year after Antoine and Louis Le Nain, yet the worlds of these urban painters could not have been more different. Vouet spent years of his artistic life in Rome, where he received a rare appointment as director of an art academy. He was recalled to Paris by Louis XIII and Richelieu and dominated the official art world of the capital city in the 1630s and 1640s. Vouet's *Presentation in the Temple* was an altarpiece for the Jesuit monastery on the Rue St. Antoine in Paris. Its patron was the Jesuit minister Richelieu, and it remained in service as an altarpiece until the French Revolution, when it was placed in the Louvre. With its brilliant colors, classical architecture, sweeping spaces, and visual drama, it contrasts in every way with the prosaic and deeply spiritual *tenebrism* of Georges de La Tour.

Born in 1602 in Brussels, Philippe de Champaigne was in Paris by 1623, working with Nicolas Poussin on the decorative paintings for the Luxembourg Palace. He was named official painter to Marie de Medici shortly thereafter and, by 1654, was a founding professor of the Académie Royale des Beaux Arts, established to educate French artists in the most sophisticated techniques of Italian and Flemish painting. A brilliant technician, de Champaigne was a deeply religious practitioner of Jansenism, a reform wing of Catholicism practiced in France until its subjugation by Louis XIV in 1679. The two paintings selected for brief discussion here represent opposite sides of his aesthetic temperament. The earlier of these paintings, *The Miracles of the Penitent St. Mary* was done in 1656 for the private apartments of Anne of Austria in the Val de Grace, and represents an obscure story from the Golden Legend. It is set in a richly detailed and beautifully conceived landscape, showing Champaigne's debt to his first master, Poussin. The second painting is a large double portrait of two Catholic sisters, the abbess and one of her charges from the Abbey of Port-Royale. Painted in 1662, it is inscribed with the identities and titles of the two women. It is referred to as *Ex Voto* (meaning "record of a vow"), and it gives an example of lifelong piety and the simple grandeur of spiritual life.

Charles Le Brun was the most influential, highly paid, and powerful artist during the reign of Louis XIV. Trained at the Académie Royale and working under Nicolas Poussin, Le Brun was discovered by Louis XIV's finance minister, Nicolas Fouquet, and commissioned to paint the interiors of Fouquet's chateau at Vaux-le-Vicomte. Louis XIV redirected the painter's work to the royal residences, and Le Brun became, with the architect Le Vau and the garden designer Le Nôtre, part of the triumvirate that designed Versailles. Le Brun became first painter to the king and, like Rubens before him, commanded a large studio of assistants who worked with him to produce a vast oeuvre. The two works selected here show the range of his career, from delightfully detailed aristocratic portraiture in his representation of the retinue of Pierre Seguier, the Chancellor of France (*Chancellor Seguier*), to the searing visual drama of the *Pietà*. ∎

Works Discussed

Georges de La Tour: *The Penitent Mary Magdalen*, 1640–1645, oil on canvas, 4'3" x 3'1".

The Card Cheat With the Ace of Clubs, 1630/34, oil on panel, 3'2" x 5'1", Kimbell Art Museum, Fort Worth, Texas, U.S.A.

The Cheat With the Ace of Diamonds, 1635, oil on canvas, 3'6" x 4'9".

The Adoration of the Shepherds, c. 1644, oil on canvas, 3'6" x 4'3".

St. Sebastian Tended by St. Irene, c. 1649, oil on canvas, 5'6" x 4'3".

St. Joseph the Carpenter, 1642, oil on canvas, 4'6" x 3'4".

Louis or Antoine Le Nain: *Peasant Meal*, 1642, oil on canvas, 3'9" x 5'3".

The Cart or *The Return from Haymaking*, 1641, oil on canvas, 1'10" x 2'4".

Philippe de Champaigne: *The Miracles of the Penitent St. Mary*, 1656, oil on canvas, 7'3" x 11'.

Ex Voto, 1662, oil on canvas, 5'5" x 7'6".

Simon Vouet: *Presentation in the Temple*, 1640–1641, oil on canvas, 12'9" x 8'3".

Charles Le Brun: *Chancellor Seguier*, 1655–1661, oil on canvas, 9'9" x 11'9".

Pietà, c. 1645, oil on canvas, 4'9" x 7'3".

Caravaggio: *The Death of the Virgin*, 1601–1606, oil on canvas, 12'1" x 8'.

Suggested Reading

Blunt, *Art and Architecture in France, 1500–1700.*

Conisbee, *George de La Tour and His World.*

Rosenberg, *France in the Golden Age.*

Questions to Consider

1. What is the painting style of Georges de La Tour? Describe his originality and choose a favorite detail in one of his paintings.

2. What was unique about the approach of the Le Nain brothers to the technique of oil painting? Describe this new kind of painting.

Claude and Poussin—French Painters in Rome
Lecture 8

It was also the century that produced two major French artists who paradoxically, and completely unlike Georges de la Tour and the Le Nain brothers, spent all of their working professional life outside of France—not just outside of Paris, but outside of France.

This lecture deals with the two artists who were, without question, the most important figures in French painting of *Le Grand Siecle* ("The Great Century"). Both of them lived relatively long and productive lives by 17th-century standards, and although each of them exerted a profound effect on painting in his native France, each spent essentially his entire working life in Rome. Beyond that geographical fact, the two were startlingly different. Nicolas Poussin was a major intellectual and spent his career among the greatest Roman patrons, poets, painters, and philosophers of his age. By contrast, Claude Lorrain was a socially simpler man, who specialized in landscape painting and who, though much admired as an artist, lacked the standing as an intellectual that was to be Poussin's calling card.

Other Works by Nicolas Poussin

In 1650, Poussin painted a self-portrait (*Self Portrait*) that is one of the most venerated images of an artist in the Louvre. Not only was Poussin widely considered to be the greatest French painter of the 17th century (and, for many, of all times), but his art is essentially impersonal and non-psychological. For that reason, it is almost surprising that he painted this self-image. We see him without artifice in his studio, wearing an elaborately folded black silk cloak over a starched white-collared shirt. He stares at us—and himself in the mirror—with steadfastness and clarity, his left hand bearing a handsome gold pinky ring and resting on a portfolio of red silk ribbon. Behind him we see the gray-framed painted panel with an inscription that identifies the artist and the date in correct Latin. Behind that is the fragment of a severely classical painting, which in turn, rests in front of another invisible painting and perhaps another.

The Plague of Ashdod is among the grimmest Old Testament scenes, and Poussin painted it relatively early in his career, in 1630 at the age of only 36. It was acquired by Louis XIV in the year of the painter's death as a testimony to the greatest French painter of the century. Ashdod, the capital city of the Philistines, was in possession of the stolen Ark of the Covenant, the single most sacred object of the Jews. God, therefore, punished them with a virulent plague, which Poussin painted with a calm determination. Not only had he had the opportunity to witness plague victims in his own life, which lends a deathly realism to the painting, but he also studied Roman sarcophagi, which are, of course, funereal sculpture. The combination of realism and solidly grounded art history make the painting particularly powerful and succeed in rooting Christianity in Roman civilization.

Echo and Narcissus is a superb example of the painter's ability to "picture" Greek mythology and to integrate the human figure into the landscape. Echo, the young nymph rendered dumb by the goddess Juno, rests alluringly amidst the rocks beside a pool, her ear cocked to hear the last words of her beloved Narcissus. Narcissus, in turn, lies dead beside the pool into which he has stared until death, his last word, "Farewell" (or *Adieux* in French), having just "echoed" throughout this quiet and melancholic landscape. Love and death are intertwined here long before Wagner.

Poussin represented *The Four Seasons* on a commission from the Duke of Richelieu, the minister of Louis XIII. They are, in effect, a grand suite of landscape paintings in which Poussin's greatness as a landscape painter is made clear. The paintings' subjects link the pagan idea of the four seasons with Christian themes in a way that is unique in the history of art. *Spring* is a representation of paradise before the fall, with Adam and Eve together in a lush landscape, in which each leaf on each tree is individually represented. In it, Eve points toward the fruits hanging from the Tree of Knowledge before picking one and feeding it to Adam. The entire course of human history is, thus, arrested, at the moment before the Fall. *Summer* is a harvest setting with the Old Testament scene of the virtuous Ruth and her future husband, Boas, while *Autumn* is an almost surreal landscape in which tiny human figures carry immense and over-scaled fruits. The perilous series is brought to a close with a completely gray representation of the *The Deluge (Winter)*, the immense Old Testament storm that eradicated virtually every creature on Earth. These four landscapes, shown alone in a single gallery, are perhaps the summit of French landscape painting in its first great century, the 17th.

The Works of Claude Lorrain

Born six years after Poussin in the fertile countryside of the French province of Lorrain, from which he took his name, Claude Gelée went to Rome in the 1620s and died there at the venerable age of 82 in 1682, almost 20 years after Poussin. In Claude's *View of the Campo Vaccino*, among the earliest paintings of his career, we see a group of northern European artists and tourists gathering in the Eternal City, which is lit by a golden light that suffuses the canvas and would become the artist's trademark. That same light fills *The Village Fête*, painted in 1639. This, together with many of Claude's landscapes, has no morally elevating subject. Rather, it represents the happy rural peoples of the Roman *campagna*, the landscapes that most French painters considered the most beautiful in the world. These simple people were painted because they descended from the ancient Romans and because they lived amidst the ruins of a great civilization.

Because pure landscape painting was considered to be too mundane to be a proper subject of great art, Claude often represented important—and, occasionally, quite obscure—mythological, historical, and religious subjects within his vast and beautifully balanced landscape spaces.

The Louvre owns two of the greatest of Claude's seascapes, in which imaginary architecture is represented in the warm light of Italy. In the earlier of the two, *Ulysses returns Chryseis to her Father*, painted in 1644, Claude represents a scene from Homer's *Iliad*. The later painting *The Disembarkation of Cleopatra at Tarsus*, of 1648, shows the destination of the Egyptian queen and mistress of a Roman emperor, after the death of Julius Caesar, to seduce his successor, Mark Antony. In each, the Sun itself glows at the center of the landscape, a pictorial device for which Claude became justly famous in his lifetime.

Perhaps the most balanced and perfectly composed of Claude's ideal landscapes in the Louvre is the *Landscape with Paris and Oenone*, which, like all the paintings by Claude with literary, mythological, or biblical subjects in the Louvre, belonged to Louis XIV. In it, one sees the famous lovers in the lower right, in an amorous scene near the end of a day whose pink light fills the painting. We know that Paris's next act will be his abduction of Helen, the act that caused the Trojan War and ended his relationship with his earlier muse, the nymph Oenone.

In each case, Claude's landscapes provide ample space for the viewer to wander—in this painting, with the aid of shepherds and their flocks—into the vast and satisfying spaces of his landscapes. Many of their earliest owners were known to "use" these landscapes as devices for calming meditation to escape the hectic pressures of life in a busy court or at the papal palace. ■

Featured Masterpiece:
The Inspiration of the Poet, Nicolas Poussin, 1630.

Nicolas Poussin was born in a small town in Normandy in 1594 and went to Paris about 1611, where he where he worked with various minor Mannerist painters and met an Italian poet, Giovan Marino, who commissioned him to illustrate Ovid's *Metamorphoses*. In 1624, Poussin arrived in Rome and, through Marino, met many important Italian patrons and intellectuals, establishing himself as a major figure in Roman intellectual life. After his completion of his only large-scale altarpiece in 1629, he neglected official commissions and worked only for private patrons who understood his aims and encouraged his forms of pictorial research.

Painted in 1630, *The Inspiration of the Poet*, is a visual evocation of literary creativity, hence taking its place in a long line of painting descending from Titian and Giorgione dealing with ambiguous literary themes. Because there is no particular literary text "illustrated" by Poussin, the painting can be read as an evocation of the sacred origins of poetic literature. At the center is not the poet but the god Apollo, who rests his arm on his gilded lyre while he dictates poetry to the listening poet. The latter figure is a young man dressed in vaguely classical garb who looks heavenward at a *putto* holding the crown of laurels that will soon crown the poet. Beneath the feet of the great god are the texts of Homer's two epic poems, the *Iliad* and the *Odyssey*, suggesting, perhaps, that Apollo is dictating the text of the *Aeneid* to Virgil and locating the ultimate origins of European literature in the great works of the ancients. The beautiful female, who appears to be a muse to both men, is actually Calliope, the muse of epic poetry. The entire painting is, at once, secular and intellectual, made, no doubt, for a world of learned men who pondered the nature of literature and its origins in classical antiquity.

It is important to note the construction of the painting as a pictorial relief based on Poussin's knowledge of Greco-Roman sculpture in the various papal and noble collections accessible to him in Rome. Rather than being placed in deep space, the figures co-inhabit a band of space very near the picture plane, almost as if evoking a relief sculpture on a sarcophagus or one of the Roman triumphal arches known to Poussin. It must also be said that Poussin was a sophisticated colorist and a fascinated observer of the effects of light on cloth, flesh, and flora.

The painting was in the collection of Cardinal Mazarin, the powerful minister for Louis XIII, by 1653. Its next appearance was in a London auction, and it spent the majority of its life in Britain, which has the most important collections of works by Poussin. It was purchased at auction in London for the Louvre in 1911 and, after its installation in the Grand Gallery, was seen by Degas, Matisse, Braque, and Picasso.

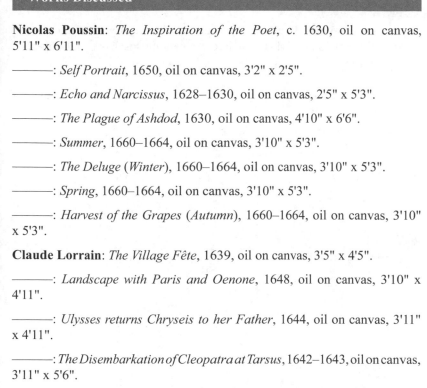

Works Discussed

Nicolas Poussin: *The Inspiration of the Poet*, c. 1630, oil on canvas, 5'11" x 6'11".

————: *Self Portrait*, 1650, oil on canvas, 3'2" x 2'5".

————: *Echo and Narcissus*, 1628–1630, oil on canvas, 2'5" x 5'3".

————: *The Plague of Ashdod*, 1630, oil on canvas, 4'10" x 6'6".

————: *Summer*, 1660–1664, oil on canvas, 3'10" x 5'3".

————: *The Deluge (Winter)*, 1660–1664, oil on canvas, 3'10" x 5'3".

————: *Spring*, 1660–1664, oil on canvas, 3'10" x 5'3".

————: *Harvest of the Grapes (Autumn)*, 1660–1664, oil on canvas, 3'10" x 5'3".

Claude Lorrain: *The Village Fête*, 1639, oil on canvas, 3'5" x 4'5".

————: *Landscape with Paris and Oenone*, 1648, oil on canvas, 3'10" x 4'11".

————: *Ulysses returns Chryseis to her Father*, 1644, oil on canvas, 3'11" x 4'11".

————: *The Disembarkation of Cleopatra at Tarsus*, 1642–1643, oil on canvas, 3'11" x 5'6".

————: *View of the Campo Vaccino*, 1636, oil on canvas, 1'10" x 2'4".

Suggested Reading

Blunt, *Poussin.*

Kitson, *Claude Lorrain.*

Oberhuber, *Poussin: The Early Years in Rome—The Origins of French Classicism.*

1. Why is Nicolas Poussin important in the history of Western art? Give details about what you like concerning his work and approach to painting.

2. Who was Claude Lorrain? Contrast his painting style with that of Nicolas Poussin.

Watteau and Chardin

Lecture 9

Following the death of Claude and Poussin in the last decades of the 17th century is that the capital of French art really did move from Rome to Paris. The Academy became stronger, and bigger, and more important.

This lecture, too, is structured as a kind of dialogue between two artists; in this case, two artists who didn't work at the same time, but in succeeding generations. These are two of the greatest French artists from the first half of the 18th century in Paris. This lecture discusses the period in the history of French art was dominated by one highly original but equally highly idiosyncratic artist, Antoine Watteau. We place Watteau's *oeuvre*, of which the Louvre possesses a virtually definitive collection, in the context of "public" artists of his generation. The lecture concludes with a discussion of the greatest 18th-century French artist in the minor genres of painting—still lifes and scenes of daily urban life. Jean-Baptiste-Siméon Chardin was 15 years younger than Watteau but equal to the older artist in aesthetic independence.

Painting in the Age of Louis XIV and the Regency

Louis XIV was involved in a continuous process of strategic wars and negotiations to enlarge the borders of France and to assert the supremacy of French power against the Spanish, the British, and the Austro-Hungarian Empire. Throughout his life, he commissioned and/or created markets for paintings representing the heroic battles that defined the contours of a new nation. This kind of painting enjoyed enormous prestige in the 17th and 18th centuries but has dropped into critical oblivion in the 20th.

Watteau Himself

No single painting by Watteau exemplifies more his aesthetic aims nor provides greater evidence of his achievements than the *The Embarkation from Cythera*, a large canvas painted in 1717. There are two versions—

another is in the Gemälde Gallerie in Berlin—but the Louvre version was accepted by the Royal Academy as Watteau's "reception piece." The painting is large and complex in its organizational structure. It represents a group of beautifully dressed courtiers who have been on an outing to the mythological island of Cythera. Watteau shows them when their idyllic day is at an end; they are saying goodbye to this temporary paradise—and to each other—as they board the boat to leave. The subtle melancholy that pervades the Paris version of the painting differentiates it from its brighter and cheerier variant in Berlin. We seem to be as much at the end of an era as an afternoon.

Watteau, *The Embarkation from Cythera*, 1717.

Watteau's *Portrait of a Gentleman* is, like many portraits in the history of art, unidentified in terms of its sitter. Whatever his name, he was clearly wealthy, well-fed, and well born. He is dressed superbly, with extensive hand embroidery on both his waistcoat and his jacket, and the sleeves of his fine cotton shirt are finished in the finest of French lace.

Although he seems to be dressed for the indoors, we see him in a darkly wild garden, leaning on what seems to be an empty pedestal and looking out of the painting to the upper right. He is, as such, full of ambiguity as a man, as a sitter, and as a painted subject.

Many of Watteau's most important and beautiful works of art are tiny easel paintings on either panel or canvas. These works were created for the incredibly luxurious but small private apartments of Parisian collectors of the period, men and women who also collected Old Master drawings and other cabinet pictures designed for the private delectation of the rich and refined.

The three paintings by Watteau selected here, *Autumn*, *The Judgment of Paris*, and *Le Faux Pas* are all small, although *Autumn* is large enough to have been included in a Salon, and each represents a scene in an intimate and deftly painted manner. Indeed, the latter two of these paintings could easily have been held in the hand of the connoisseur, who could pass it from friend to friend.

Featured Masterpiece:
Pierrot, Jean-Antoine Watteau, 1718–1719.

A portrait of an actor? A portrait of a comedian? A portrait of a clown? Pierrot was a stock character in the *commedia dell'arte*, a traditional Italian form of burlesque that came to France in the late 17th century.

Born in the provincial town of Valenciennes, which vacillated between France and Flanders in the 17th century, Antoine Watteau was a journeyman artist who never married and had little formal education. Yet his personality and intelligence were such that he befriended many aristocrats and members of the wealthiest bourgeoisie in Paris. Did he think of himself as a sort of aesthetic "Pierrot"? Is this a self-portrait?

In painting this huge work, Watteau chose to ennoble an anonymous individual who assumes the identity of a clown named Pierrot. Hence, it is a portrait of a "character" rather than an individual, thereby raising fascinating questions about its function. Tradition tells us that the painting served as a public sign for a picture dealer in the early years of the 18th century, and several have argued that it actually was intended to serve a similar purpose by Watteau himself, who often attended performances of popular street theater. We see Pierrot standing alone on a hillock facing the viewer. Beneath him, as if below a stage, are other actors dressed in diverse costumes, as well as a ruffed figure riding a donkey. The whole painting confronts the viewer with a mystery that has yet to be solved.

Jean-Baptiste-Siméon Chardin

Chardin is among the most original painters of the entire 18th century. Although rigorously trained in the Academy and successful in terms of sales, critical notices, and collecting, his works looked like no other painter of his generation, and he stuck steadfastly to the minor pictorial subjects of still-life, genre, and on rare occasions, portraiture. None of his sitters was truly of social importance, and his paintings of French life record that of the Parisian middle class rather than aristocrats or members of the *haute bourgeoisie*. The Louvre's collection of paintings and pastels by Chardin is unparalleled, and it is a pity to reduce such a great and original artist to four works. As we talk about him, we see him looking steadfastly at us—as he did at himself in a mirror—in his pastel *Self Portrait*, done in the 1770s, at the end of his life, when he found it difficult to work in oil.

The Ray, Chardin's largest and most ambitious still-life painting is also his most unusual. Painted as a reception piece for the Academy, it was most likely completed in 1726, when Chardin was 28 years old. Shown on a crowded kitchen table in what must be the home of a comfortably middle-class or wealthy Parisian, we see a large ray, a fish much prized in French cooking, hanging by a hook, its glistening entrails displayed for the viewer. Next to this hideously gorgeous fish, we see a black and white cat, snarling with its back arched, at this spectacle of edible delights. The oysters, onions, crockery, cloth, copper, silver, pewter—all these variously light-absorptive materials are arranged masterfully by Chardin so that the still-life becomes almost an altar to the visible and tactile qualities of ordinary edible objects. It is no accident that Denis Diderot, the greatest art critic of the time, recommended that other painters study this work in detail. Nor is it a coincidence that it was copied by Cezanne and Matisse.

Throughout the 1730s and 1740s, Chardin alternated between the patient recording of carefully arranged still lifes and the painting of figural genre, in which he analyzed the lives and mores of middle class Parisians. Though small in scale, these paintings have a conceptual and compositional grandeur that was completely original in 18th-century French painting.

Here, we shall examine two, beginning with *The Kitchen Maid* of 1739, which represents a handsome young woman who has gone shopping for her Parisian mistress. She returns home with meat, held in a fold of plain white cloth, and two huge loaves of bread, which she has placed on a kitchen sideboard as she walks into the room. The interplay of the utterly mundane subject and the sublime arrangement of forms, textures, volumes, and values is masterful and was recognized by many early connoisseurs of painting. It is no accident that Chardin's paintings were much prized by contemporary collectors, even by aristocrats, and that his paintings sold particularly well to sophisticated Parisian collectors who had already discovered Dutch 17th-century art.

Chardin, *The Kitchen Maid*, 1739.

The second genre scene is entitled *The Young Draftsman*, which is another kind of painting than *The Kitchen Maid*. First of all, the canvas is larger, so that the figure is virtually life size in representation, rather than "miniaturized" for the aesthetic delectation of her social betters. Here, we see an artist who is so young that we take him to be an apprentice or student. He is well-dressed and self-possessed but is unaware that he is being painted, staring instead with rapt attention at his drafting tool, a piece of white chalk held in a handmade wooden splice, which he appears to be whittling with the knife in his other hand. What we see here is far from the "inspiration" that Fragonard will later show. Instead, the young artist is a journeyman, more interested at this stage in his tools than in aesthetic results. Again, the mundane material realities of art become the subject for a thoughtfully and artfully composed visual investigation of the nature of art making. ■

63

Jean-Antoine Watteau: *Pierrot*, also known as *Gilles*, 1718–1719, oil on canvas, 6'1" x 4'11".

————: *Portrait of a Gentleman*, c. 1715–1720, oil on canvas, 4'3" x 3'2".

————: *The Embarkation from Cythera*, 1717, oil on canvas, 4'3" x 6'4".

————: *Autumn*, 1715, oil on canvas, 1'7" x 1'4".

————: *Le Faux Pas* (*The Mistake*), 1716–1718, oil on canvas, 1'3" x 1'.

————: *The Judgment of Paris*, 1720–1721, oil on panel, 1'6" x 1'.

Jean-Baptiste-Siméon Chardin: *The Ray*, 1725–1726, oil on canvas, 3'8" x 4'9".

————: *Self Portrait*, 1771, pastel on vellum, 1'5" x 1'3".

————: *The Young Draftsman*, 1737, oil on canvas, 2'8" x 2'1".

————: *The Kitchen Maid*, 1739, oil on canvas, 1'6" x 1'3".

Suggested Reading

Connisbee, *Painting in 18th-Century France.*

Michel, *Chardin.*

Posner, *Antoine Watteau.*

Questions to Consider

1. Why does the Louvre have the definitive collection of Antoine Watteau's work? Who was he, and what is his role in the history of French painting?

2. What is so original about the work of French artist Jean Simeon Chardin? Use specific examples from the paintings we have studied to support your thoughts.

Boucher, Fragonard, and the Rococo in France
Lecture 10

Francois Boucher and Jean-Honoré Fragonard, two artists who were a generation apart from each other and who dominated the exciting visual sensibility that we now call today, and that was in fact called in the 18th century, the "Rococo."

French painting during the reign of Louis XV was dominated by two artists of two different generations whose informal, erotically charged painting has come to be called *Rococo*. Painting for the court and for wealthy urban clients of both the aristocracy and the bourgeoisie, Boucher and Fragonard tackled mythological, religious, historical, and real-life subjects with an apparent ease that belies their sophisticated training and their knowledge of the history of art. This lecture considers their achievement in terms of the Louvre's superb collections and in the context of the work of their predecessors and followers.

François Boucher

In 1725, the great French academic painter François Lemoyne sent to the Academy a superb painting, *Hercules and Omphale*, representing the Greek god Hercules and his mortal friend Omphale at the ecstatic point at which they have "exchanged clothing," and she, the queen of Lydia, has become the god's mistress. The erotic luxury of the painting—its lack of any elevating moral quality—shows just how far French painting and connoisseurship had come since the establishment of the Academy in the late 17th century. Lemoyne truly set the stage for the Rococo.

Boucher, *Le Dejeuner* (*The Luncheon*), 1739.

Boucher was 23 years old when he saw Lemoyne's painting at the Salon and was already fully launched in a career that lasted until 1770. He so dominated French painting between 1730 and 1770 that no one else could match the range of his subjects, commissions, and private wealth. Living, like most great artists, in the Louvre, then in a large house acquired through his own wealth, Boucher was the epitome of success in the Parisian art world of the 18th century. A family man and a hard worker, he never had the intellectual aims of such artists as Watteau or Fragonard and can be thought of as a brilliantly talented journeyman of painting.

At the end of his third decade, he painted a huge canvas, *Venus Requesting Arms for Aeneus from Vulcan*. This oppositional painting—male-female, heat-cool, fire-air, hard-soft, ruddy-white, Earth-heaven—presents a scene from classical mythology with no clear moralizing lesson. Its assurance and ease of execution separate it from the more labored compositions of Lemoyne, and the painting was acquired by no less a patron than King Louis XV himself.

In 1739, Boucher painted a small canvas with the unprepossessing title *The Luncheon*. The painting is as charmingly informal in its composition and chromatic structure as paintings by Chardin are controlled and rigid, and we see the aesthetic of Boucher at work. It represents a young Parisian family having lunch in their luxurious urban apartment. The large, multi-paned windows tell us that it is an older house, probably in the Marais or on the Ile St. Louis, but the family is prosperous enough to have redecorated it in the last several years with new paneling and Rococo furniture. We see a father and mother with their two children and a nanny or attendant who holds the baby, taking their coffee or chocolate in front of the fire on a brilliantly sunny day. Boucher himself was 36 in 1739 and already had children, yet we have no inclination to think that we are in Boucher's own home—he separates himself from the scene with all the devices of a practiced maker of illusions.

In 1742, Boucher painted a small masterpiece called *Diana Leaving the Bath*. It was exhibited at the Salon of that year, hanging at eye level because of its small dimensions. In it, we see one of the first of the "liberated women goddesses," Diana. As the birds in the lower right corner and the dogs slathering noisily in the water indicate, she has just come from a successful hunt and has decided to bathe with her attendant before a meal. Unlike the voluptuously heavy women of Rubens and even Lemoyne, the bodies of Boucher's Diana and attendant are trim, athletic, and lithe without losing some of the charming layers of softer skin. It is little accident that this seems to have been Renoir's favorite painting throughout his life, and we must remember that, as a child, he lived in the crowded slum that was torn down for the enlargement of the Louvre in the Second Empire.

The Rape of Europa is a subject painted by scores of artists in the history of Western art, and the Louvre itself has at least 30 paintings of the scene. Boucher painted the subject in several formats at different moments in his career, but the Louvre's large and fully realized version was owned by the king himself. We see the mortal Europa, a princess of exceptional beauty, who is spied by the Greek god Jupiter while she plays at the beach with the ladies of her court. Jupiter assumes the form of a pretty white bull, speaks softly to her, and persuades her to mount him before he takes her, crying, into the water to the island of Crete. Boucher shows us all the dramatic tension in the scene with the wind-whipped foliage at the left, the strong surges of the sea and its tritons, and the interplay of clouds and sun. It is a wonderful romp through mythology with Boucher with no need for Latin or Greek!

Featured Masterpiece:
Figure de Fantasie:
Portrait of the Abbé de Saint-Non or *Inspiration*,
Jean-Honoré Fragonard, 1769.

With this painting, we see the agitated, spontaneous performance of an artist who wants us to virtually witness him in the act of painting. The colors are mixed as he rushes to complete a section of the sleeve; the skin tones of the face don't blend but are, rather, juxtaposed touches of wet paint applied on wet. The inscription (on the reverse) tells us that the painting represents the Abbé de Saint-Non and that it was painted in an hour! Scholars believe that the inscription is not in the artist's hand but was added later.

It has also been called *Inspiration* and *Figure de Fantasie*, the latter title in keeping with a group of other similarly sized and composed figure paintings by Fragonard, all painted in the same rapid style. Fragonard invited his friends to his studios to watch him paint. These works, the so-called "Fantasy Portraits," represent friends of the painter and evoke the world of his studio, where friends would don costumes, use studio props, and "pose" for the master. The true subject of this and the artist's other paintings is art itself, its intimacy and spontaneity. In addition, Fragonard infuses these works with a kind of active informality and virtuosity that are the true hallmarks of Rococo painting in France.

This great painting, as well as many other masterpieces of French Rococo art, came to the Louvre via the La Caze bequest in 1869. The room built specifically for the bequest was visited by every great French artist of the late 19th and early 20th centuries and actually painted by Edouard Vuillard. One can easily imagine the young Manet or Renoir standing enrapt in front of this Fragonard.

Jean-Honoré Fragonard

Born in 1732 in the south of France in the town of Grasse, known for its perfumes, Fragonard was a generation younger than the famous Boucher. Fragonard's greatness as his true successor did not materialize until after Boucher's death in 1770, when Fragonard was 38 years old.

When the painter was in his early 30s, he began work on his first masterpiece, *The High Priest Coresus Sacrifices Himself to Save Callirhoe*, his reception piece for membership in the Academy. The subject he chose was of daunting obscurity and moral complexity, involving unrequited love, revenge, madness, and a double suicide, all set in remote classical antiquity. The young artist chose to represent the scene on a huge scale—more than 9 by 12 feet—set in the smoky darkness of a temple of Bacchus. The painting almost emits the scents of pagan antiquity. The scene chosen by Fragonard was a climactic moment in which the priest Coresus plunges the dagger of sacrifice into himself, rather than into his intended victim, Callirhoe. She faints in an erotic swoon beside him, knowing that the lover she had earlier spurned has made the ultimate sacrifice for her.

Lest we worry that it would be his fate to reinvent history painting from the erotic charms of Boucher, we need only to look at the most deliciously free representation of female sexuality in the history of French art, Fragonard's *The Bathers*. It was never included in a Salon, so the painting has been variously dated by scholars. Whatever its date, the work eschews mythology altogether. We see no contemporary clothing or jewelry to interrupt our adoration of these gloriously athletic young bathers. Unlike Boucher's chaste and calm Diana, Fragonard's girls leap in an erotic frenzy of excitement, and the entire painting, like the later Fantasy Portraits, seems to have been frothed up in one sitting without interruption for a drink, a nap, or a meal.

There is no more ravishing and erotic representation of sexual relations in the history of art than Fragonard's *The Bolt*, of 1778. It represents an utterly salacious scene without literary or mythological context. We see a beautiful young couple; the raven-haired young man, clad only in his underwear, grasps a seemingly willing young blonde woman, yet to be disrobed. A forlorn apple is, with the bolt, the only "prop" in the room, and reminds us that, whenever sex occurs, there is always a faint echo of the first sexual encounter in history and its cause, the apple from the Tree of Knowledge.

Fragonard's Contemporaries

Fragonard's brilliance was so blazing that few attempted to compete with him, but Jean-Baptiste Greuze and Hubert Robert worked in his wake, staking out more modest territories for specialization.

Greuze, who became the favorite painter of the greatest writer-critic of 18th-century France, Diderot, worked carefully on his paintings, infusing contemporary life with a rigor lacking in Fragonard. *The Punished Son* from the Salon of 1778 represents a thoroughly middle-class family at a moment of domestic crisis, when a contemporary "Prodigal Son" comes home to find his father dead, while his sisters mourn aggressively and his mother remonstrates.

Hubert Robert became one of the most popular and prolific painters of ruins in the history of art, working in Italy, France, and in czarist Russia, where he painted numerous scenes of Italian antiquity. We see him here in a portrait (*Hubert Robert*) by his friend, the great female artist Elisabeth Vigée-Lebrun, whose husband was an art dealer in 18th-century Paris. Robert's own *Imaginary View of the Grande Galeries in Ruins* appeared in the Salon of 1796. Here, one sees Robert applying the lessons he learned from the Roman ruins of Italy to post-revolutionary contemporary France. All civilizations will decline and die, and we must imagine their achievements in ruin in order to understand them in life. ■

Works Discussed

Jean-Honoré Fragonard: *Figure de Fantasie: Portrait of the Abbé de Saint-Non* or *Inspiration*, 1769, oil on canvas, 2'7" x 2'2".

————: *The Bolt*, c. 1778, oil on canvas, 2'5" x 3'1".

————: *The Bathers*, 1772–1775, oil on canvas, 2'1" x 2'7".

————: *The High Priest Coresus Sacrifices Himself to Save Callirhoe*, c. 1765, oil on canvas, 10'2" x 13'1".

François Boucher: *Le Dejeuner* (*The Luncheon*), 1739, oil on canvas, 2'8" x 2'2".

————: *Diana Leaving the Bath*, 1742, oil on canvas, 1'10" x 2'5".

————: *The Rape of Europa*, 1747, oil on canvas, 5'3" x 6'4".

————: *Venus Requesting Arms for Aeneas from Vulcan*, 1732, oil on canvas, 8'3" x 5'9".

Elisabeth Vigée-Lebrun: *Hubert Robert*, 1788, oil on panel, 3'5" x 2'9".

François Lemoyne: *Hercules and Omphale*, 1724, oil on canvas, 6' x 4'11".

Jean-Baptiste Greuze: *The Punished Son*, 1778, oil on canvas, 4'3" x 5'4".

Hubert Robert: *Imaginary View of the Grande Galeries in Ruins*, 1796, oil on canvas, 3'9" x 4'9".

Anthony van Dyck: *Venus Asking Vulcan for Arms for Aeneas*, c. 1630, oil on canvas, 8'9" x 6'9".

Suggested Reading

Conisbee and Bailey, *The Age of Watteau, Chardin, and Fragonard: Masterpieces of French Genre Painting.*

Crow, *Painters and Public Life in 18ᵗʰ-Century Paris.*

Hyde, *Making Up the Rococo: François Boucher and His Critics.*

Sheriff, *Fragonard: Art and Eroticism.*

Questions to Consider

1. Explain the French Rococo style. How do the paintings of Jean-Honoré Fragonard exemplify Rococo?

2. Compare Fragonard and Boucher. What are the similarities and the differences between these two artists? Discuss this topic in light of the paintings presented in this lecture.

Jacques-Louis David and His School
Lecture 11

In France, there was one painter who actually lived through all of that time, embodied its values, and notions, and questions in countless masterpieces, and who is probably the most important pictorial recorder of political upheaval, political regeneration, moral questioning about the rights of citizens and the rights of the individual of any painter in human history.

In this lecture, we concentrate on the definitive collection of paintings in the Louvre by the greatest French painter from 1780–1820, Jacques-Louis David. A brilliant success as a student, an academician in Rome, a star in the final Salons of the *Ancien Regime*, a member of the revolutionary government, director of the Louvre, Napoleon's "court painter," and finally, an exile from post-Napoleonic France in Belgium, David was the dominant painter of his generation in Europe and one of the greatest teachers in the history of art. We will study his career, as well as several of his great pupils, Gros, Prud'hon, and Girodet.

Jacques-Louis David

Born in 1748 and raised in Paris, David learned to paint under the watchful eye of the elderly Boucher. He was trained in the atelier of Vien and sent as a young genius to Rome. We see a characterization of David as an artist in his *Self-Portrait* of 1894 in the Louvre. There exists a strong relationship between painting and governmental politics at volatile times in the history of Europe. The *Self-Portrait* was painted when the artist was already famous, after the death by guillotine of Louis XVI and as David was beginning to reorganize the royal collections for the public.

The Oath of the Horatii of 1784, painted five years before the *Brutus*, represents three young men, the sons of Horatio, who took an oath in the 7th century B.C. to fight to the death for Rome, just as a group of youths from the Curiatus family made a similar oath for their city, Alba. The painting deals with issues of war, patriotism, family loyalties, and politics and is a strident display of sexism, in which men and women play roles that are utterly at odds with each other. The women respond emotionally to their brothers' oaths, although one of them is conflicted because she is engaged to one of the Curiatus brothers, whom they will fight to the death. The painting derives from the theater rather than from "real" history, in this case the tragedy *Horace* by Pierre Corneille.

In 1799, as the republican government began to reform itself after the bloody Reign of Terror and a good deal of sectarian violence, David painted his largest work to date: *The Sabines*. Although other painters (notably Poussin) had represented the abduction of the Sabine women by Roman troops needing wives, David had become a pictorial harbinger of peace in 1799 and elected to represent a completely different scene. In this painting, the Sabine women, many of whom had become Romans and produced Roman children, intervened in the senseless destruction in the war between the Romans and Sabines, using a kind of nonviolent protest later practiced by the likes of Gandhi and Martin Luther King, Jr. For the first time in David's art, women play an active role in politics, and the central figure of "action" in this essentially military painting is female, her arms outstretched like those of the Horatii, but in an imploring rather than a martial gesture.

David, *Madame Recamier*, 1800.

In 1800, David was commissioned to paint the most beautiful young society woman of Paris, Madame Recamier, daughter of a wealthy banker from Lyon, wife of an older— and wealthier—Parisian banker (*Madame Recamier*). Madame Recamier was the reigning beauty of her day, but she was vain enough that she played painters off against each other, posing simultaneously for David and his pupil Gerard. David posed her in a startling simple empire dress with little of the trappings of luxury with which she was usually associated. She reclines alertly on a classically inspired wood settee in an interior empty of everything but a candleholder and a small footrest. The painting has a kind of scrubbed gestural surface, indicating that it was left unfinished, and David is reported to have told the sitter that his own whim was to leave her forever "unfinished." The Louvre bought the painting from David's estate sale in 1826. The famous sitter never owned it.

On December 2, 1804, Napoleon was consecrated as emperor of France in Notre Dame Cathedral by the pope, who was brought to Paris for the occasion. The emperor commissioned the greatest living French painter to record the occasion in a huge painting with life-size figures, which was intended to surpass Rubens's coronation of Marie de Medici. It took David and his assistants more than three years to finish the immense painting the *Consecration of Napoleon I*, which was first exhibited in the Salon Carrée in the Louvre in 1808. In it, David represents Napoleon crowning Josephine, as empress.

Featured Masterpiece:
The Lictors Bringing to Brutus the Bodies of His Sons,
Jacques-Louis David, 1789.

Painted for the Salon, then held in the Louvre, this painting became a signal cry for reform in pre-revolutionary Paris in the months before the storming of the Bastille in July of 1789. Just 31 at the time, David was already a painter with brilliant originality who had returned to Paris triumphantly from his studies in Rome. The painting represents an obscure scene from early republican Rome, a scene that required explanation for most contemporary viewers and, for that very reason, elicited the interest of critics, writers, other artists, and officials of the royal government. David derived much of the impetus for the painting from his reading of Voltaire's play *Brutus* of 1730.

The play is about Lucius Junius Brutus, the first consul of republican Rome, who discovers that his two sons are plotting against the republic, favoring the return of an aristocratic family, the Tarquins. When he hears of their deaths, Brutus takes the news stoically, knowing that, for him, the future of his people and their freedom from tyranny is more important than the lives of his corrupt sons.

In a visual tour of the painting, we see the feet of the two sons on the left behind the seated figure of Brutus, along with a section of his house dominated by an allegorical sculpture of Rome. To the right, separated from the father, are the entwined bodies of Brutus's wife and their daughters, who scream, gesture, and cry in an anguish that Brutus himself stoically avoids. David uses color, composition, contour, and space to make visually manifest these two responses to the tragedy. The painting clearly affected public discourse—novels, pamphlets, the theater, and criticism—creating a climate in which the very existence of the monarchy was questioned by an artist who had been trained by the government and who displayed his work in an exhibition it sponsored.

The Pupils of David

Baron Antoine-Jean Gros was, among David's many pupils, the one who achieved the most official success with Napoleon's government. He became the greatest painter of Napoleon's numerous military victories throughout the world, and even today, every French schoolchild learns of the military campaigns of the greatest French general from the paintings of Gros. In 1799, Napoleon defeated the Middle Eastern city of Jaffa, where he is shown by Gros visiting a hospital for victims of the plague in *Napoleon Visiting the Pest House at Jaffa*. Unafraid of the disease, utterly human, and in an odd way, heroic, Napoleon dominates the painting as a healer as much as a general.

Pierre-Paul Prud'hon was born in Cluny, near the famous monastic church, 10 years later than David. As an artist, he was fascinated by the *sfumato* of masters from the High Renaissance, such as Leonardo and Andrea del Sarto, and developed an almost moonlit style with deep velvety shadows and mysteriously enveloping contours. His famous portrait of *The Empress Josephine* was painted as the childless beauty began to realize her fall from power, seated in a garden at dusk, contemplating its shadows. Even Prud'hon's masterful *Justice and Divine Vengeance Pursuing Crime* of 1808 (reworked in 1814), commissioned for the Palace of Justice in Paris, has a proto-Romantic nocturnal quality, as if the crime interested the artist as much as the heroic allegorical figures that attempted to defeat it.

Anne-Louis Girodet-Trioson was the most brilliant technician and perhaps the most precociously talented artist in David's circle. *The Sleep of Endymion* of 1814 is perhaps the most chastely erotic painting ever made and a pictorial essay in androgyny that has made it the darling of historians of sexuality. This gorgeous young man, a shepherd who was purportedly the grandson of Jupiter, is spied by the Moon, who requests from the great god that he grant Endymion eternal youth through sleep. As viewers, we gaze with rapt eyes educated by Girodet at the young man, who sleeps in art as he does in myth. ∎

Works Discussed

Jacques-Louis David: *The Lictors Bringing to Brutus the Bodies of His Sons*, 1789, oil on canvas, 10'7" x 13'10".

———: *The Oath of the Horatii*, c. 1784, oil on canvas, 10'10" x 13'11".

———: *Self-Portrait*, 1794, oil on canvas, 2'8" x 2'1".

———: *The Sabines*, 1799, oil on canvas, 12'8" x 17'2".

———: *Madame Recamier*, 1800, oil on canvas, 5'10" x 8'.

———: *Consecration of Napoleon I*, 1805–1808, oil on canvas, 20'4" x 32'1".

Baron Antoine-Jean Gros: *Napoleon Visiting the Pest House at Jaffa*, 1804, oil on canvas, 17'5" x 23'7".

Pierre Paul Prud'hon: *Justice and Divine Vengeance Pursuing Crime*, 1808, oil on canvas, 8' x 9'8".

————: *The Empress Josephine*, 1805, oil on canvas, 8' x 5'10".

Anne-Louis Girodet-Trioson: *The Sleep of Endymion* or *Effet de lune* (*Effect of the Moon*), 1791, oil on canvas, 6'6" x 8'7".

Nicolas Poussin: *The Rape of the Sabines*, 1637–1638, oil on canvas, 5'3" x 6'9".

Suggested Reading

Crow, *Emulation: Making Artists for Revolutionary France.*

Herbert, *David, Voltaire, Brutus and the French Revolution.*

Solomon-Godeau, *Male Trouble.*

Questions to Consider

1. Who was Jacques-Louis David and what accounts for his supremacy during the late 18th century in France?

2. What is the legacy of Jacques-Louis David? Use examples from his artwork and the artwork of his pupils to argue your case.

Delacroix and Ingres—The Great Dialectic

Lecture 12

The art of the late 18th century and early 19th century was dominated by one great artist and his students, an artist whose sensibility, in fact, transformed itself to include the extraordinary transformations in French society, French art, and French politics.

In this lecture, we will look at the most important paintings in the Louvre by the two artists who defined French art in the first half of the 19th century, Eugène Delacroix and Jean-Auguste-Dominique Ingres. The extreme contrast in their styles, imagery, and artistic aims demonstrates the dialectical structure of French society in the generations after the French Revolution. This lecture reads their art in both sociopolitical and aesthetic terms and considers it in the context of the painting of Théodore Géricault, the greatest precursor of Delacroix.

Jean-Auguste-Dominique Ingres

Born in provincial Montaubon in the south of France, Ingres received his early training under Jacques-Louis David, while he served stints in Rome both as a student and, eventually, as the director of the French Academy in Rome. He believed in art as rooted in the Greco-Roman tradition and its pictorial revivals in the Italian Renaissance.

Three portraits of Monsieur and Madame Philibert Rivière and their daughter (*Philibert Rivière*; *Madame Rivière*; *Mademoiselle Caroline Rivière*) were painted by Ingres in 1805–1806 and exhibited at the Salon of 1806 before the painter's departure for Rome. The artist was 26 years old when he represented the family, and these portraits were truly "debut" performances for a young artist working in what was then still republican France. Painted in 1826 for the ceiling of the Salle Clarac in the Louvre, *The Apotheosis of Homer* has, since 1827, been hung as an easel painting and acts as the supreme personification of classical intelligence. In it, one sees the conservative Ingres creating an image of a stabile, ideal world of important artists, writers, composers, and philosophers. Each of these figures contributes to a collective view of culture with its roots in the Greek epics of Homer, the first "writer" of Western history, whose two great works, the *Iliad* and the *Odyssey*, are personified as women at the poet's feet. Included in the painting are Ingres' heroes as an artist, particularly Raphael (whose hand is held by Apelles), Michelangelo, and Poussin. Missing are Leonardo, Rubens, Rembrandt, Velasquez—indeed, any Italian, French, Flemish, or Dutch painter who worked outside the classical cannon.

There is nothing to say that the classical world was uninterested in the erotic, and even the most "correct" of Neoclassical artists, Ingres, was susceptible to the pliant beauties of the idealized female body. Two of his greatest representations of the nude are the *Large Odalisque* of 1814 (commissioned by Napoleon's sister) and *The Turkish Bath* from 1862. Both provide ample proof of his notion that beauty itself is embodied in the female form and the best way to have access to that form is to create an imaginary and rather chaste harem or *seraglio* populated only by women. A rapid tour of these marmoreal surfaces with their gorgeous props—feathered fans, pearl jewelry, and slave bracelets—harks back to the Barberini *Hermaphrodite* in the Louvre and to the contemporary sculpture of the Italian artist Canova.

Théodore Géricault

Théodore Géricault was born in Rouen, the capital of upper Normandy, and trained, like Ingres, in Paris and Rome. Because his life was short and his talent seemingly unfocused until the last decade of his 43 years, his *oeuvre* is comparatively small. His masterpiece, *The Raft of the Medusa*, exhibited at the Salon of 1819, is a work that truly changed the course of modern painting. Instead of representing an event from classical history, as David had done, or ennobling a scene from the military victories of Napoleon, in the manner of Baron Gros, Géricault decided to represent on an immense scale a scene from a contemporary event involving incompetence, human misery, and possibly, cannibalism. This painting set the stage for a kind of art in which the miseries of the victims of history were given precedence over the glories of the generals, kings, and emperors.In preparation for his greatest painting and as part of his larger artistic project, Géricault visited morgues, hospitals, and asylums to study the artistic physiognomy of death, depression, insanity, and disease. His painting *The Madwoman* was conceived by him as a portrait in the manner of Rembrandt's portraits of nameless common people, but this time with an edge.

Eugène Delacroix

Delacroix was trained as an artist in the very same manner as Ingres, but his interests, education, and temperament were completely different. We see him as a noble visionary, open to improvising and inventing new forms rather than channeling the artistic greatness of others. Delacroix made his debut as an artist in the Salon of 1822 with *The Barque of Dante*, a darkly Romantic and morbid representation of the young Dante being rowed into the Inferno in a boat alongside his "guide," Virgil. Here, the journey of classicism is the opposite of that later ennobled by Ingres. The troubled Roman poet and his "modern" companion, Dante, were unafraid of danger, death, and depravity, and the writhing figures in the water remind us of both Rubens and Michelangelo, both easily visited by Delacroix in the Louvre. Virtually every great painter in later French art, including Manet, Degas, and Cezanne, copied this painting.

One of Delacroix's largest and most important paintings is *The Death of Sardanapalus* of 1827. Rather than chose as his subject a morally elevating scene from ancient history, as had David, Delacroix ransacked contemporary Romantic literature, this time a long poem by the British poet Lord Byron. The scene is one of violent murder in the court of an Assyrian king, who reclines passively on a vast bed in the shadows, contemplating the rape and murder of his concubines and exotic courtiers and guards that he had ordered. Criticized as chaotic and formless by most of the critics, it is the most enigmatic and, for that reason, the most challenging of Delacroix's history paintings.

In 1832, Delacroix was sent to Morocco as part of the official French delegation of the Count de Mornay. While there, he filled sketchbooks, made numerous watercolors, and began a lifelong project of what one might called anthropological Orientalism—the representation of the exotic Middle East based on visual fact. *The Women of Algiers in their Apartment* was a great hit in the Salon of 1834, where its contrast with the Orientalizing female figures of Ingres was surely noticed. It represents demurely clad young women, presumably in a harem, served by a flouncing black eunuch, who exits "stage right." Delacroix stressed less the eroticism of the harem than its exotic décor and psychic subtlety. The painting was copied or quoted by many great artists, including Renoir, Matisse, and Picasso, and is, in some ways, the most popular work in Delacroix's *oeuvre*.

Very few great French artists actually got the chance to "decorate" the Louvre, and one of them was Delacroix. When Napoleon III, with his architects Visconti and Lefuel, began their painstaking reconstruction and completion of the Louvre, transforming it into the museum it is today, they sought early on to restore the great Gallery of Apollo, designed by the same architect and decorated by the same painters, Le Vau and Le Brun, who worked on Versailles under the same monarch, Louis XIV. Because the room had been severely damaged, a central portion of the ceiling painting by Le Brun was destroyed, and in 1851, at the height of his fame, Delacroix was commissioned by the state to "complete" the room with a decoration related to Louis XIV, the Sun King, and his association with Apollo, *Apollo Vanquishing the Python*. Here, Apollo is not the serenely confident rider of the chariot that brings the Sun around the Earth but is, rather, a mighty hero who wards off the evil of a vast writhing python. The coils of the python and the athletic strength of Apollo bring a Rubenian energy into this masterful classical room, something unknown to Le Brun. ■

Featured Masterpiece:
Liberty Leading the People on the 28th of July, 1830, Eugène Delacroix, 1830.

Taking a visual tour of the painting, we see the location in Paris (the church of Notre Dame in Paris is clearly visible to the right of center), and the class, gender, and age of its major figures (all working class, all male, and mostly young). Note the forward thrust of the painting—the figures move strongly toward the viewer, rather than laterally or back into space, making the painting active and aggressive rather than contemplative.

The Street Revolution of 1830 was the first of three periodic Paris-based revolts in the 19th century to follow patterns set by the 1789 Revolution. An idea of France as a country lurching between two political, aesthetic, and social extremes was established—one associated with a hereditary monarchy, the Church, and patriarchal authority based on tradition and the second rooted in the concept of human rights of common citizens, equality of the sexes, and the emotional freedom of the individual. One was visually associated with Classicism; the other, with the emotionally charged rhythms of a kind of Neo-Baroque style then called Romanticism.

Who was Eugène Delacroix, and why was he in Paris during the 1830 Revolution? Delacroix's life included early training and regular trips to England. He had interests in literature and music and was a participant in the newly budding Romantic movement that swept Northern Europe in the period. He was interested in the nexus of history and the contemporary world; he believed that contemporary life was "living history" and that the role of the great artist was both to make history "live" for contemporary viewers and to consolidate images of contemporary history for posterity. *Liberty* is an example of the latter. Delacroix's drawings of the revolt illustrate his decision to be an "eyewitness to history."

"Liberty" is represented allegorically as a classical woman. The painting relates to the *Venus de Milo*, discovered in 1820, though with strong differences, and prefigures the *Victory of Samothrace*, which was not discovered until 1863. The painting was exhibited in the Salon of 1831 and purchased immediately by the state. Given its charged political imagery, it was not displayed until 1848, when the next short-lived republican government rethought the Louvre.

Eugène Delacroix: *The Barque of Dante*, 1822, oil on canvas, 6'2" x 8'1".

————: *The Death of Sardanapalus*, 1827, oil on canvas, 12'10" x 16'3".

————: *Liberty Leading the People on the 28th of July, 1830*, 1830, oil on canvas, 8'6" x 10'8".

————: *The Women of Algiers in their Apartment*, 1834, oil on canvas, 5'11" x 7'6".

————: *Apollo Vanquishing the Python*, central panel from the Gallery of Apollo, 1850–51, mural painting, 26'3" x 24'7".

Jean-Auguste-Dominique Ingres: *Philibert Rivière*, 1805, oil on canvas, 3'10" x 2'11".

————: *Madame Rivière*, 1806, oil on canvas, 3'10" x 2'11".

————: *Mademoiselle Caroline Rivière*, 1805, oil on canvas, 3'3" x 2'4".

————: *La Grande Odalisque*, 1814, oil on canvas, 3' x 5'4".

————: *Death of Leonardo*, 1818, oil on canvas, 1'4" x 1'8", Musée du Petit Palais.

————: *The Apotheosis of Homer*, 1826, oil on canvas, 12'8" x 16'10".

————: *The Turkish Bath*, 1862, oil on panel, 3'7" x 3'7"

Théodore Géricault: *The Raft of the Medusa*, 1819, oil on canvas, 16'1" x 23'6".

————: *The Madwoman*, c. 1822, oil on canvas, 2'6" x 2'1".

Suggested Reading

Novotny, *Painting in Europe, 1780–1880*.

Prideaux, *The World of Delacroix*.

Rosenblum, *Ingres*.

Wright, *The Cambridge Companion to Delacroix*.

1. Compare and contrast the painting styles of Delacroix and Ingres. How are they different? What is new and fresh about their styles?

2. What were the sociopolitical implications of the paintings of Delacroix and Ingres? Take examples from the paintings that we have examined in this lecture.

Visiting the Louvre

1. The Italian side of the Louvre is the most heavily visited and should be seen either first thing in the morning or in the evening, when the museum has fewer visitors.

2. The north side can be visited virtually anytime, because it is not as heavily frequented and has works of equal quality. However, in the evening, there is none of the glorious natural light that so animates this great urban palace.

3. Visitors going for the first time should plan to see the museum in two or three half-day visits punctuated with other site-seeing in Paris.

4. Visitors to the Louvre should have a guidebook, the best English guide is the widely available *Gallimard Guide to the Louvre.*

5. Many people who are unaccustomed to museum visits tend to look at everything in each room and become fatigued after an hour or so. The best way to visit a section of a museum is to stroll through and scan a number of galleries quickly. Then, you select which two or three works of art in each gallery to spend time with as you walk backward or review the galleries.

Visiting the Galleries of European Paintings

1. There is no "right way" to look at paintings. Most Americans have been taught to think of paintings in terms of the artist's composition, color distribution, and manipulation of pictorial space. This way of looking stresses the "form" of the painting at the expense of the subject. It is important, in looking carefully at works of art, to think about the relationship between the formal qualities of the work and its subject matter. The "content" of a picture is a fusion of the two.

2. When studying a work of art, spend at least two minutes scanning the entire surface, then at least as much time looking at particularly complex or detailed areas of the painting. It is better to spend four or five minutes with one or two works in a gallery than to scan every painting. After entering a room, scan it in less than 30 seconds and choose one or two works to study in greater detail.

3. Walk quickly from one room to the next and stroll through several galleries (five to seven) before planning a room-to-room visit.

4. You can never see everything, so don't even try. If you feel overwhelmed, leave immediately. A good rule of thumb is to plan a first visit to the Louvre as if it will be the first of many.

5. Visiting a great museum is a strenuous endeavor requiring the expenditure of physical, mental, and emotional energy. In a way, it is not unlike climbing a mountain: The better prepared you are, the greater your success and the more you will savor your accomplishment. If they are great, works of art are difficult and ambiguous rather than easy, and the more you bring to them, the more they will repay your attention.

Looking at the *Mona Lisa*

1. Study the *Mona Lisa* in reproduction before going to the museum, and make several decisions about what you want to observe carefully from the original itself. Then, join the group in front of the painting and think about its scale, frame, relationship to the viewer, and other basic questions as you approach it.

2. When you finally stand in front of the painting, have a clear idea of one or two aspects of it that you want to verify from the original, such as the position of the hands, the color and disposition of the eyes, the smile, the relationship between the figure and the landscape, the pathways into the landscape, or the time of day evoked by the painter.

Timeline: Louvre History

1180–1223 .... Reign of Philippe Auguste.

1190 .... Philippe Auguste leaves for the
Crusades and commands the creation of
a rampart to enclose and protect the city.
A royal fortress protected citizens from
possible attack along the Seine. This is
the birth of the Louvre.

1358 .... Paris Rebellion. Charles V orders
a second wall around the Louvre
for protection.

1515–1547 .... Reign of François I. His collection of
paintings is kept at Fontainebleau. He
begins changes to Louvre.

1528 .... François I demolishes the Great Tower
of Philippe Auguste.

1546 .... Architect Pierrre Lescot is
commissioned by François I to create
a new wing to replace part of the
medieval rampart.

1547–1559 .... Reign of Henri II.

1566 .... Henri II's widow, Catherine de Medici,
orders the Tuileries Palace to be
constructed. Architect Philibert Delorme
and sculptor Jean Goujon collaborate.

1774	Comte D'Angiviller (1730–1809) is made the Royal Director of Buildings. His goal is to create a royal museum at the Louvre for the public.
1774–1792	Reign of Louis XVI.
July 14, 1789	Storming of the Bastille.
August 10, 1792	Collapse of the monarchy.
1793	The Louvre opens as the Central Museum of the Arts, a national museum, on the first-year anniversary of the fall of the monarchy.
1802	Vivant Denon is appointed director of the museum.
1803	The Louvre is the Musée Napoleon. Napoleon's treasures are displayed.
1815	The downfall of Napoleon results in the return of most art.
1830	July Revolution.
1848	Baron Haussmann demolishes the districts surrounding the Louvre. Architect Visconti plans the new Louvre. (1852–1870 Second Empire.)
1852	Lefluel and Visconti work on new designs for the Louvre.
1870	Napoleon III's Louvre is finished. End of the Second Empire.

1871.. On May 23, the Tuileries and the
Palais-Royal are burned down.
Paris Commune.

1939.. Museum Director Henri Verne hides the
works of art in Chambord, transporting
them to various chateaux.

1981.. The "Grand Louvre" is planned by
President Mitterand.

1989.. Architect I. M. Pei's Pyramide opens.

1998.. The "Grand Louvre" is completed.

Timeline:
Lives of Major Artists Featured at the Louvre

c. 1395–1441 .... Van Eyck, Jan.

c. 1399–1464 .... Van der Weyden, Roger.

c. 1400–1455 .... Fra Angelico.

c. 1430/1431–1506 .... Mantegna, Andrea.

1452–1519 .... Leonardo da Vinci.

c. 1465–1530 .... Metsys, Quentin.

1471–1528 .... Dürer, Albrecht.

1475–1564 .... Buonarroti, Michelangelo.

1483–1520 .... Raphael (Raffaello Sanzo).

c. 1485–c. 1540 .... Clouet, Jean.

1497–1543 .... Holbein the Younger, Hans.

c. 1488–1576 .... Titian (Tiziano Vecellio).

c. 1510–1572 .... Clouet , François.

c. 1510–c. 1565 .... Goujon, Jean.

1512–1594 .... Tintoretto (Jacopo Robusti).

1619–1690.................................... Le Brun, Charles.

1620–1694.................................... Puget, Pierre.

1629–1667.................................... Metsu, Gabriel.

1629–1684.................................... Hooch, Pieter de.

1632–1675.................................... Vermeer, Johannes or Jan.

1684–1721.................................... Watteau, Jean-Antoine.

1688–1737.................................... Lemoyne, François.

1699–1799.................................... Chardin, Jean Siméon.

1703–1770.................................... Boucher, François.

1722–1808.................................... Hubert, Robert.

1725–1805.................................... Greuze, Jean-Baptiste.

1732–1806.................................... Fragonard, Jean-Honoré.

1733–1808.................................... Robert, Hubert.

1737–1824.................................... Girodet de Roucy-Trioson, Anne-Louis.

1746–1828.................................... Goya y Lucientes, Francisco de.

1748–1825.................................... David, Jacques-Louis.

1755–1842.................................... Vigée-Le Brun, Elisabeth-Louise.

Glossary

Academy: The term used for institutions that taught classical art and technique; as Academies developed, many became dogmatic and conservative, which restricted artistic expression and style.

Altarpiece: An altarpiece is a work of art, commonly a series of panel paintings or sculptures, designed to be placed behind, above, or on an altar.

Annunciation: The biblical event in which the Angel Gabriel announces to the Virgin Mary that she will bear the Christ child, born of the Holy Spirit.

Apocrypha: The books containing such narratives as Judith and Susanna that were included in the Catholic Old Testament but were not included in the Hebrew or Protestant Old Testament canons.

Baroque: Refers to a highly ornamental and flamboyant artistic style that began in Italy and spread across Europe from the late 1500s through the 1700s.

Book of hours: A typically illuminated book of prayer developed according to a set calendar and time schedule used for devotion.

Chiaroscuro: This Italian word describes the arrangement of light and dark elements in a pictorial representation.

Classicism: A word referring to Greek or Roman art or to artwork that was later derived from or inspired by Greek or Roman art.

Duomo: The Italian word for "cathedral."

Eucharist: The Church sacrament in which consecrated bread and wine are consumed during the ceremony of communion, which symbolizes Christ's sacrifice on the cross.

Fresco: The art of painting on wet plaster.

Frieze: A frieze is a horizontal band made up of sculpture or painting that runs along the wall of a room, normally just below the ceiling.

Genre: *Genre* is used in art to describe subjects drawn from everyday life.

Gothic: The medieval artistic style of music, sculpture, and architecture during the Middle Ages, specifically Europe from the 12th through the 15th centuries.

Humanism: A cultural and intellectual movement during the Renaissance that resulted from the rediscovery of the arts and philosophy of the Greeks and Romans.

Mannerism: A stylized approach to art that dominated Italy and spread throughout Europe in the 16th century. Mannerism is characterized by dramatic color, distortion of anatomy, and ambiguous subject matter.

Naturalism: This term is used to describe realistic or exact depictions of objects or figures, in contrast to idealized or stylized representations.

Neoclassicism: Term used to define the "new" Classicism, or the rediscovery of the art and style of classical antiquity. In reaction to the Baroque and Rococo, Neoclassicism offered a return to the classical aesthetic of the Greeks and Romans.

Pietà: The word *pietà*, literally "pity" in Latin, is used for the visual portrayal of the body of the dead Christ lying in the lap of the grieving Virgin Mary.

Polyptych: A series of two or more painted or sculpted panels that are usually hinged together. The term is typically used for works with three or more parts.

Predella: Smaller panels on the sides or lower part of an altarpiece that given added narrative to the main part of the altarpiece.

Realism: Term used for the style of depiction of life as it actually appears, most notably in subjects of everyday life or the ordinary.

Reformation: The religious movement of the 1500s in which the practices and beliefs of the Catholic Church were challenged, giving birth to the Protestant Church.

Renaissance: The literal translation of *Renaissance* means "rebirth" in Latin. Lasting from the 1400s through the 1600s, the term describes the period of Humanistic revival that began in Italy and traveled throughout Europe and was characterized by a renewed interest in classical art, literature, and architecture.

Rococo: A style that developed under Louis XV of France and extended across the rest of the European continent; it was a reaction to the Baroque.

Romanesque: A style of architecture or art that began in 11th-century France and spread throughout Europe; it draws its inspiration from Roman architecture and style.

Romanticism: Term used to characterize the artistic movement of the late 18th and early 19th centuries, which was a reaction to the strong rationalism of the Enlightenment. It is characterized by strong emotion, ideology, individual achievement, respect for nature, and the historical representations of ideas.

Tempera: A water-based paint in which ground colors or pigments are most often "tempered," or suspended in egg yoke.

Triptych: A series of three paintings. Usually a triptych is religious in theme for use as an altarpiece or in devotion.

Trompe l'oeil: In French, this term means to "fool the eye." It is used to describe a painting or a portion of a painting in which the artist attempts to deceive the viewer into thinking that the objects depicted are real.

Biographical Notes

Boucher, François (Paris, 1703–Paris 1770). A French Academy painter, he came to exemplify the rococo in his decorative and ornamental style.

Buonarroti, Michelangelo (Caprese, 1475 - Rome, 1564). Considered to be one of the most important artists in history, Michelangelo was accomplished in the areas of sculpture, architecture, and painting.

Caravaggio, Michelangelo Merisi (Caravaggio, 1570–Porto Ercole, 1610). Revolutionary in his approach in dramatically contrasting light and dark, Caravaggio was a painter of realistic naturalism.

Chardin, Jean Siméon (Paris, 1699–Paris 1799). An 18th-century French painter, he was known for depicting still life and genre subject matter of the bourgeois.

Cimabue (Cenni di Pepe) (Florence, c1240–Florence, after 1402). An Italian painter from Florence, he broke with the Byzantine style for a more realistic approach that ushered in the Renaissance style.

Clouet, François (Unknown–Paris, 1572). Son of Jean Clouet, he was a 16th-century French court painter whose work was characterized with a Florentine naturalism.

Clouet, Jean (c1485–c1540). Court painter of Francois I of France, he represented his subjects in a Renaissance style of idealism.

David, Jacques-Louis (Paris 1748–Brussels 1825). Representing the Neoclassical style, David painted works that demonstrated support for French nationalism and Napoleon.

Delacroix, Eugene (Charenton-Saint-Maurice, 1798–Paris 1863). The great French romantic painter, his work was characterized by its strong use of color in treating historical, literary, and contemporary subjects.

Dürer, Albrecht (Nürnberg 1471–Nürnberg 1528). The great German master, Dürer, was the consummate Northern Renaissance painter, printmaker, and draughtsman.

Dyck, Anthony van (Antwerp, 1599–Blackfriars, 1641). Student of Rubens, this painter from Antwerp was one of the great Flemish artists of the 17th century.

El Greco (Domenico Theotocopoulos) (Candia, 1541–Todedo, 1614). "The Greek," El Greco was the great master of the Spanish school of painting in the Mannerist style.

Eyck, Jan van (Maaseyck, ?–Bruges 1441). Credited with perfecting the use of oil painting, this Flemish artist was characterized by his religious and portrait works on panel.

Fra Angelico (Vicchio di Mugello?, c 1400–Rome, 1455). A Dominican monk, Fra Angelico was a gothic artist who depicted religious themes and subjects.

Fragonard, Jean-Honoré (Grasse, 1732–Paris, 1806). Trained by Chardin and Boucher, the French artist Fragonard painted in the rococo style.

Giotto di Bondone (Colle di Vespiganano, c1267–Florence, 1337). Pupil of Cimabue, the Florentine Giotto was the first great artistic genius of the Italian Renaissance.

Goya y Lucientes, Francisco de (Fuendetodos, 1746–Bordeaux, 1828). The Spanish court painter, Goya was an artist known for his portraiture and whose political and social depictions became the basis of modern realism.

Gros, Baron Antione-Jean (Paris 1771–Meudon 1835). Educated by Jacques Louis David, Gros was a French neoclassical painter who excelled in historical subjects such as the campaigns of Napoleon.

Hals, Frans (Antwerp, c1581–Haarlem, 1666). The Flemish painter Hals was the first great artist of the Dutch School in the 17th century, he was best known for his fine portraiture.

Holbein the Younger, Hans (Augsburg, 1497–London, 1543). The Bavarian Renaissance artist, Holbein was gifted in painting and printmaking and later became the court painter of Henry VIII in England.

Hooch, Pieter de (Rotterdam, 1629–Amsterdam, 1684). Dutch Baroque painter, Hals was a genre painter of the Delft School.

Ingres, Jean-Auguste-Dominique (Montauban, 1780–Paris, 1867). The Neoclassicist painter Ingres, student of Jacques Louis David, was the great French artist of the portrait as well as the religious and mythological.

Le Brun, Charles (Paris, 1619–Paris, 1690). Known for decorated the insides of Versailles, Le Brun was an accomplished decorative artist of 17th-century France.

Le Nain, Louis or Antoine (Laon, c 1600/1610–Paris, 1648). Two artist brothers from 17th-century France, the Le Nain were innovative in their genre painting of every day life in France.

Leonardo da Vinci (Vinci, 1452–Cloux, 1519). The great Italian master artist, Leonardo was the ultimate Renaissance man being elegantly accomplished as an inventor, sculptor, architect, and painter.

Lorrain, Claude Gellée (Chamagne, 1600–Rome, 1682). The 17th-century French painter from Lorrain, Claude Gellee was renowned for his landscapes.

Mantegna, Andrea (Isola di Carturo, c1430/1431–Mantua, 1506). From Padua and Mantua, Mantegna was the great Italian master painter who developed space and perspective in his works.

Murillo, Bartolomé Esteban (Seville, 1618–Seville, 1682). The great 17th-century Spanish painter, Murillo primarily painted Biblical or religious themes and on occasion genre themes of every day life.

Poussin, Nicolas (Les Andylys 1594–Rome 1665). Poussin was the great French classicist who painted religious and mythological subjects, as well as landscapes.

Raphael (Raffaello Sanzo) (Urbino, 1483–Rome, 1520). The renowned Florentine, originally from Urbino, Raphael was one of the great Italian Renaissance painters.

Rubens, Petrus-Paulus (Siegen, 1577–Antwerp, 1640). Known for his use of vibrant color and use of light, Rubens was the great Flemish Baroque painter.

Titian (Tiziano Vecellio) (Pieve di Cadore, c1488–Venice, 1576). Called the greatest Venetian Renaissance painter, this student of Giorgione was known for his bold and rich use of color with expressive brush work.

van Rijn, Rembrandt Harmensz (Leiden, 1606–Amsterdam, 1669). One of the great artists in history, Rembrandt was a Dutch painter who was a portrait artist and created scenes Biblical, mythological, and historical narratives.

Vermeer, Johannes or Jan (Delft, 1632–Delft, 1675). Very little is known about this Dutch genre painter who was known for his sensitive treatment of both light and color.

Veronese, Paolo (Paolo Caliari) (Verona, 1528–Venice, 1588. Born in Verona, but active as a Venetian painter, he was one of the great Italian decorative painters.

Watteau, Jean-Antoine (Valenciennes, 1684–Nogent-sur-Marne, 1721). This French rococo artist painted figures in romanticized and idealized settings.

Weyden, Roger van der (Tournai, c1399–Brussels, 1464). A mid-15th-century painter, he was Flemish painter from the Netherlands.

Zurbarán, Francisco de (Fuente de Cantos, 1598–Madrid, 1664). A 17th-century Spanish artist, he was known for primarily religious themed paintings.

Bibliography

Alpers, Svetlana. *The Art of Describing Dutch Art*. Chicago: University of Chicago Press, 1983. The best political history of Dutch art.

Bazin, Germain. *Louvre Masterpieces of Italian Painting*. New York: New York Graphic Society, 1956. No one has surpassed Bazin's knowledge of the Italian collection at the Louvre.

———. *The Museum Age*. New York: Universe Books, 1967.

Berger, Robert W. *The Palace of the Sun: The Louvre of Louis XIV*. Penn State University Press, 1993. The clearest discussion of the Louvre as a palace.

Blunt, Anthony. *Art and Architecture in France, 1500–1700*. New Haven: Yale University Press, 1999. Still the standard for the study of the art of France.

———. *Poussin*. New York: Knowledge Publications, 1917. This is the best survey of Poussin's work and his role in Roman intellectual life.

Bonfante-Warren, Alexandra. *The Louvre*. New York: Barnes & Noble, 2000.

Bresc-Bautier, Geneviève, ed. *Louvre: The Collection*. Paris: Editions de la Réunion des musées nationaux, 1991.

———. *The Louvre: An Architectural History*. New York: Rizzoli, 1995.

Brown, Christopher. *Rembrandt*. New Haven: Yale University Press, 1991. Brown's book is the most easily accessible and complete Rembrandt survey.

———. *Van Dyck*. Oxford: Phaidon, 1982. Van Dyck was the most important pupil of Rubens, and he took these art techniques abroad.

Brown, Jonathan. *The Golden Age of Painting in Spain*. New Haven: Yale University Press, 1991. No American scholar has done more for Spanish painting in the last generation than Jonathan Brown.

Carrier, David. *Museum Skepticism: A History of the Display of Art in Public Galleries*. North Carolina: Duke University Press, 2006. A persuasive discussion of the art museum, with special attention to the Louvre.

Clark, Kenneth. *Leonardo da Vinci*. London: Penguin, 1981. Clark produced one of the greatest accounts of an artist's life ever written.

Conisbee, Philip. *Georges de La Tour and His World*. Washington, DC: National Gallery of Art, 1996. Conisbee has written the a definitive exhibition catalogue.

————. *Painting in 18th-Century France*. Ithaca, NY: Cornell University Press, 1981. A superb and accurate account of 18th-century French painting.

Conisbee, Philip, and Colin B. Bailey. *The Age of Watteau, Chardin, and Fragonard: Masterpieces of French Genre Painting*. New Haven: Yale University Press, 2003. Read this book for an accurate understanding of this period.

Cox-Rearick, Janet. *Musée Du Louvre: La Collection de Françoise I*. Paris: Editions des musées nationaux, 1972. This book is the definitive account in English of the earliest great French royal art collection.

Crow, Thomas E. *Emulation: Making Artists for Revolutionary France*. New Haven: Yale University Press, 1995. This book is the clearest and most recent study in English of revolutionary France and its artists.

————. *Painters and Public Life in 18th-Century Paris*. New Haven: Yale University Press, 1985. A fiercely intelligent study of the politics of painting in Paris during the 18th century.

Cuzin, Jean-Pierre. *The Louvre : French Paintings*. London: Scala, Paris and Philip Wilson Publishers, 1982.

D'Archimbaud, Nicholas. *Louvre: Portrait of a Museum*. New York: Abrams, 2001.

Freedberg, Sydney. *Painting in Italy, 1500–1600*. New Haven: Yale University Press, 1993. This is the definitive account of Italian Renaissance painting.

Gaborit, Jean-René. *The Louvre: European Sculpture*. London: Scala, 1994.

Gowing, Lawrence. *Paintings in the Louvre*. New York: Stewart, Tabori, and Chang, 1987.

Guide Guillimard. *The Louvre*. Paris: Editions Nouveaux-Loisirs/Editions de la Réunion des musées nationaux, 1994.

Herbert, Robert. *David, Voltaire, Brutus and the French Revolution*. New York: Viking Press, 1973. The most intelligent discussion of a single masterpiece connected with the French Revolution.

Hyde, Melissa Lee. *Making Up the Rococo: François Boucher and His Critics*. Los Angeles: Getty Press, 2006. The book is a savage but intelligent criticism of the French aristocratic art of the mid-18th century.

Kitson, Michael. *Claude Lorrain*. Washington, DC: The National Gallery of Art, 1969. Kitson is the most probing scholar of Claude Lorrain.

Kubler, George. *Art and Architecture in Spain and Portugal*. London: Penguin, 1959. This is the most profound survey of the Golden Age of Spanish art.

Laclotte, Michel. *The Louvre: European Paintings, Artists Outside France*. Italy: Scala Publications, 1989.

Laclotte, Michel, and Cuzin, Jean-Pierre. *The Louvre: European Paintings*. Italy: Scala Publications, 1997.

McClellan, Andrew. *Inventing the Louvre: Art, Politics, and the Origins of the Modern Museum in Eighteenth-Century Paris*. Berkeley: University of California Press, 1999. This is the best book in English on the origins of the Louvre as a museum. I consider this essential reading.

Michel, Marianne Roland. *Chardin*. London: Thames and Hudson, 1996. The book is an excellent and reasoned monograph.

Mignot, Claude. *The Pocket Louvre: A Visitor's Guide to 500 Works*. New York: Abbeville, 2000.

Millen, Ronald, and Robert Wolf. *Heroic Deeds and Mystic Figures: A New Reading of Rubens' Life of Maria de'Medici*. Princeton, NJ: Princeton University Press, 1998. The most complete account in English.

Oberhuber, Konrad. *Poussin: The Early Years in Rome—The Origins of French Classicism*. Hudson Hills, NY: The Kimbell Art Museum, 1988. Although eccentric in its methods, this book is profoundly stimulating.

Pasquier, Alain. *The Louvre: Greek, Etruscan, and Roman Antiquities*. Paris: Editions Scala, 1991.

Posner, Donald. *Antoine Watteau*. Ithaca, NY: Cornell University Press, 1984. This is a balanced and thorough account of the artist's career and life.

Prideaux, Tom. *The World of Delacroix*. New York: Time Library, 1966. If you can find this old classic, you will not be able to put it down.

Quiniam, Pierre. *Louvre: The Visit*. Paris: Editons de la Réunion des musées nationaux, 1997.

Rosenberg, Pierre. *France in the Golden Age*. New York: Metropolitan Museum of Art, 1982. Use this book as a guide to local paintings of the great era.

Rosenblum, Robert. *Ingres*. New York: Abrams Press, 1990. Although it looks like a picture book, this is the best monograph on Ingres.

Sahut, Marie Catherine. *Le Louvre d'Hubert Robert*. Paris: Éditions de la Réunion des musées nationaux, 1979.

Schama, Simon. *The Embarrassment of Riches: An Interpretation of Dutch Culture in the Golden Age*. Berkeley: Random House, 1988. No one has written a more important cultural account of Dutch painting.

Sheriff, Mary D. *Fragonard: Art and Eroticism*. Chicago: University of Chicago Press, 1990. This book offers a stimulating perspective on Fragonard and his art.

Smart, Alistair. *The Dawn of Italian Painting, 1250–1400*. Oxford: Phaidon, 1978. The most accessible account of the independent easel picture in Italy.

Solomon-Godeau, Abigail. *Male Trouble*. New Haven: Yale University Press, 1997. *Male Trouble* is a provocative book about the crisis of sexuality and painting in post-revolutionary France.

Stratton-Pruitt, Suzanne. *Bartolome Esteban Murillo (1617–1682): Paintings from American Collections*. New York/Fort Worth: Abrams/ Kimbell Art Museum, 2002. Use this as a guide to Spanish painting in your local museum.

White, Christopher. *Peter Paul Rubens: Man and Artist*. New Haven: Yale University Press, 1987. A clear and precise account of Rubens's career.

Wright, Beth S., ed. *The Cambridge Companion to Delacroix*. Cambridge Press, 2001. Wonderfully intelligent and accessible collection of Delacroix's writings.

Zerner, Henri. *Renaissance Art in France: The Invention of Classicism*. Paris: Flammarion, 2003. The best writer on French Renaissance art of this generation.

Ziegler, Christiane. *Louvre: Egyptian Antiquities*. Paris: Editions Scala, 2004.

Notes

Notes

Notes

Notes

Notes

Notes